P9-DWH-941

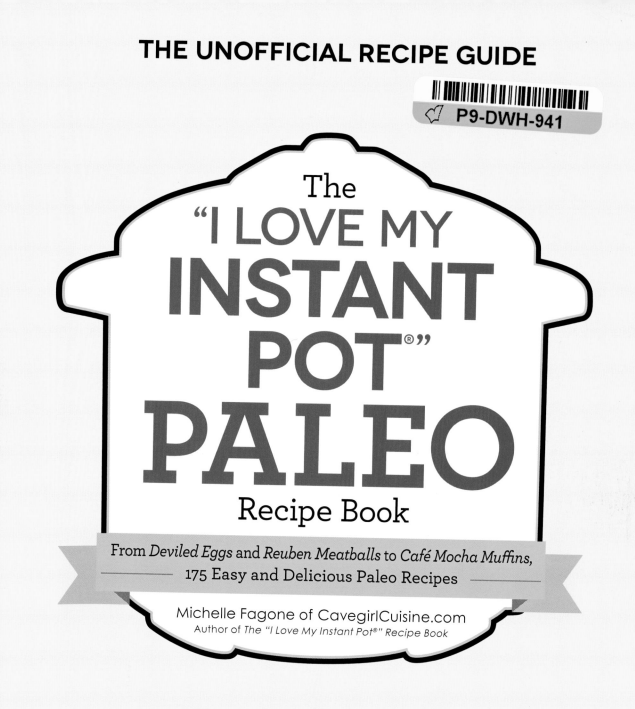

The "I LOVE MY INSTANT POT®"
PALEO
Recipe Book

From *Deviled Eggs* and *Reuben Meatballs* to *Café Mocha Muffins*,
175 Easy and Delicious Paleo Recipes

Michelle Fagone of CavegirlCuisine.com
Author of The *"I Love My Instant Pot®" Recipe Book*

Adams Media
New York   London   Toronto   Sydney   New Delhi

To Samantha and Calla

THANK YOU for all the laughs in the kitchen and complete honesty over my creations.

I love you, Mom

Adams Media
An Imprint of Simon & Schuster, Inc.
57 Littlefield Street
Avon, Massachusetts 02322

First Adams Media trade paperback edition DECEMBER 2017.

ADAMS MEDIA and colophon are trademarks of Simon and Schuster.

For information about special discounts for bulk purchases, please contact Simon & Schuster Special Sales at 1-866-506-1949 or business@simonandschuster.com.

The Simon & Schuster Speakers Bureau can bring authors to your live event. For more information or to book an event contact the Simon & Schuster Speakers Bureau at 1-866-248-3049 or visit our website at www.simonspeakers.com.

Interior design by Colleen Cunningham
Photographs by James Stefiuk

Manufactured in the United States of America

10 9 8 7 6 5 4 3 2 1

Library of Congress Cataloging-in-Publication Data
Fagone, Michelle, author.
The "I love my Instant Pot®" paleo recipe book / Michelle Fagone of CavegirlCuisine.com, author of "The 'I love my Instant Pot®' recipe book".
Avon, Massachusetts: Adams Media, 2017.
Series: "I Love My".
Includes index.
LCCN 2017031651 (print) | LCCN 2017037760 (ebook) | ISBN 9781507205747 (pb) | ISBN 9781507205754 (ebook)
LCSH: Pressure cooking. | Electric cooking. | High-protein diet--Recipes. | Gluten-free diet--Recipes. | Prehistoric peoples--Nutrition. | Cooking (Natural foods) | BISAC: COOKING / Methods / Special Appliances. | COOKING / Specific Ingredients / Meat. | COOKING / Courses & Dishes / General. | LCGFT: Cookbooks.
LCC TX840.P7 (ebook) | LCC TX840.P7 F335 2017 (print) | DDC 641.5/87--dc23
LC record available at https://lccn.loc.gov/2017031651

ISBN 978-1-5072-0574-7
ISBN 978-1-5072-0575-4 (ebook)

Contains material adapted from the following title published by Adams Media, an Imprint of Simon & Schuster, Inc.: The "I Love My Instant Pot®" Recipe Book by Michelle Fagone, copyright © 2017, ISBN 978-1-5072-0228-9.

Contents

Introduction

The paleo diet (or lifestyle, as I like to think of it) has become increasingly popular in the past several years, but that doesn't mean it is a "fad" diet. Eating paleo just means eating real, whole, and unprocessed foods. One of the most significant benefits of adhering to a paleo lifestyle is the potential for decreasing your risk of developing a number of chronic diseases such as cancer, diabetes, cardiovascular disease, and osteoporosis.

Also known as the caveman diet, the term *paleo* refers to a time when people ate only grass-fed game, wild-caught fish, nuts, vegetables, berries, and occasionally, other fruits. These people lived before the time of modern agriculture and the domestication of animals. When they needed meat, they hunted, and they gathered berries and nuts. There were no grains planted in fields and no milk past the weaning stage. Subsequently, the population wasn't plagued by many of the diseases that plague humans today.

Even though they had to forage, hunt, and kill most of their food, Paleolithic humans ate better-quality food than most of the world does today. Not only are the hundreds of quick-fix weight-loss products wreaking havoc on the human body, but the standard American diet (SAD)—with grains at the helm—is believed to contribute to a number of diseases caused by inflammation.

You may be thinking that you need to move to a forest and take up hunting, fishing, and gardening to be on today's paleo diet, right? That couldn't be further from the truth. This lifestyle simply requires a shift in your thinking. First, you will need to learn what foods are considered paleo "yes" foods and paleo "no" foods. From there, all you need to start on your journey toward paleo success is a simple shopping list, an open mind, and a whole bunch of recipes! While cooking paleo may seem intimidating in the beginning, the truth is that many of the recipes adored by families the world over can easily be converted to paleo-friendly options with a few carefully chosen ingredients and some fun substitution. When it comes to cooking paleo, it's all about getting creative.

And that's where your Instant Pot® comes in. Cooking with an Instant Pot® is a life-changing experience, especially when you follow the Paleolithic lifestyle. This multifunction cooking tool allows you to sauté, brown, steam, and warm your food. It cooks soups, eggs, and even cakes! And the high-pressure cooking and steaming ability of an Instant Pot® does wonders to steaks, pork shoulders, and chicken. With the touch of a button you'll be able to cook cuts of meat that would normally take hours in just minutes. The Instant Pot® cooks food at a low temperature but it does it more efficiently than other slow-cooking methods or appliances because it also uses pressure and steam. It is like a pressure cooker and a slow cooker rolled into one. This cooking method also seals in essential vitamins and minerals and allows the Instant Pot® to turn out healthier, better-tasting food that is perfect when you're on the go.

Whether you've just bought your Instant Pot® or have been using one for years and just need some inspiration, this book is for you. Inside you'll find 175 delicious paleo recipes ranging from Pumpkin Chip Muffins and White Chicken Chili to Tender Flank Steak with Mushrooms and Onions and Steamed Mussels and Chorizo. You'll also find decadent desserts, including Double Chocolate Custard and Upside-Down Chocolate Cherry Cake. The more you cook, the more you'll realize how versatile the Instant Pot® really is, whether you're making a hearty breakfast, an amazing main course, or a delicious dessert. So plug in your Instant Pot® and get ready to enjoy some amazing, delicious, and quick paleo meals.

1

Cooking with an Instant Pot®

So you're about to venture into the amazing world of Instant Pot® cooking...but you're not sure where or how to start. Don't worry, this chapter will give you the information you need to know to get started. Here you'll learn what all those buttons on your Instant Pot® do, how to release the pressure from the Instant Pot® when the cooking time is up, how to keep your Instant Pot® clean, and more.

Even though you'll learn all this information in this chapter, it's important that you read the owner's manual as well. The user manual is your key to successfully creating the recipes throughout this book. In addition to pointing out the basic functions of the appliance, it will tell you to do an initial test run using water to get familiar with the Instant Pot®. I can't stress enough that you need to do this. It will familiarize you with this appliance and take away some of the anxiety. In addition, this first run will help steam-clean your pot before you use it to make a favorite recipe.

But for now, let's take a look at some Instant Pot® basics.

Function Buttons

You are staring at the Instant Pot® and there are so many buttons. Which one should you use? Most of the function buttons seem obvious, but it is important to note that several are set with preprogrammed default cooking times. Also, keep in mind that every button option on the Instant Pot® is programmed with a 10-second delay, meaning that cooking begins 10 seconds after you hit the button. Most likely you will utilize the Manual or Pressure Cook button the most because you are in complete control, but read on for more detailed information on the remaining function buttons.

Manual/Pressure Cook button. Depending on the model of Instant Pot®, there is a button labeled either Manual or Pressure Cook. This might be the most used button on the Instant Pot®. The default pressure setting is High; however, you can toggle the pressure from High to Low by pressing the Pressure button. Use the Plus and Minus buttons to adjust the pressurized cooking time.

Sauté button. This button helps the Instant Pot® act as a skillet for sautéing vegetables or searing meat prior to adding the remaining ingredients of a recipe, and it is used for simmering sauces as well. There are three temperature settings—Normal, Less, and More—that can be accessed using the Adjust button. The Normal setting is for sautéing, the Less setting is for simmering, and the More setting is for searing meat.

Keep the lid open when using the Sauté button to avoid pressure building up.

Soup button. This button is used to cook soups and broths at high pressure for a default of 30 minutes. The Adjust button allows you to change the cooking time to 20 or 40 minutes.

Porridge button. This button is used to cook porridge, congee, and jook in the Instant Pot® at high pressure for a default of 20 minutes. The Adjust button allows you to change the cooking time to 15 or 40 minutes.

Poultry button. This button is used to cook chicken, turkey, and even duck at high pressure for a default of 15 minutes. The Adjust button allows you to change the cooking time to 5 or 30 minutes.

Meat/Stew button. This button is used to cook red meats and stew meats at high pressure for a default of 35 minutes. The Adjust button allows you to change the cooking time to 20 or 45 minutes.

Bean/Chili button. This button is used to cook dried beans and chili at high pressure for a default of 30 minutes. The Adjust button allows you to change the cooking time to 25 or 40 minutes.

Rice button. This button is used to cook white rice such as jasmine or basmati at low pressure. The Instant Pot® will automatically set the default cooking time by sensing the amount of water and rice in the cooking vessel.

Multigrain button. This button is used to cook grains such as wild rice, quinoa, and barley at high pressure for a default of 40 minutes. The Adjust button allows you to change the cooking time to 20 or 60 minutes.

Steam button. This button is excellent for steaming vegetables and seafood using your steamer basket. It steams for a default of 10 minutes. The Adjust button allows you to change the cooking time to 3 or 15 minutes. Quick-release the steam immediately after the timer beeps so as to not overcook the food.

Slow Cook button. This button allows the Instant Pot® to cook like a slow cooker. It defaults to a 4-hour cook time. The Adjust button allows you to change the temperature to Less, Normal, or More, which correspond to a slow cooker's low, normal, or high. The Plus and Minus buttons allow you to adjust the cooking time.

Keep Warm/Cancel button. When the Instant Pot® is being programmed or it is in operation, pressing this button cancels the operation and returns the Instant Pot® to a standby state. When the Instant Pot® is in the standby state, pressing this button again activates the Keep Warm function.

Automatic Keep Warm function. After the ingredients in the Instant Pot® are finished cooking, the pot automatically switches over to the Keep Warm function and will keep your food warm up to 10 hours. This is perfect for large cuts of meat as well as soups, stews, and chili, allowing the spices and flavors to really marry for an even better taste.

The first digit on the LED display will show an L to indicate that the Instant Pot® is in the Keep Warm cycle, and the clock will count up from 0 seconds to 10 hours.

Timer button. This button allows you to delay the start of cooking up to 24 hours. After you select a cooking program and make any time adjustments, press the Timer button and use the Plus or Minus keys to enter the delayed hours; press the Timer button again and use the Plus or Minus keys to enter the delayed minutes. You can press the Keep Warm/Cancel button to cancel the timed delay. The Timer function doesn't work with Sauté, Yogurt, and Keep Warm functions.

How Does Food Cook in 0 Minutes?

If you are confused about how some recipes require "0" minutes to cook, it's not a typo. Some veggies and seafoods that only equire minimal steaming are set at zero cooking time. Food can actually be cooked in the time that it takes the Instant Pot® to achieve pressure.

Locking and Pressure-Release Methods

Other than the Sauté function, where the lid should be off, or the Slow Cook or Keep Warm functions, where the lid can be on or off, most of the cooking you'll do in the Instant Pot® will be under pressure, which means you need to know how to lock the lid before pressurized cooking and how to safely release the pressure after cooking. Once your ingredients are in the inner pot of the Instant Pot®, to lock the lid put

the lid on the Instant Pot® with the triangle mark on the lid aligned with the Unlocked mark on the rim of the Instant Pot®. Then turn the lid 30 degrees clockwise until the triangle mark on the lid is aligned with the Locked mark on the rim. Turn the pointed end of the pressure release handle on top of the lid to the Sealing position. After your cooking program has ended or you've pressed the Keep Warm/Cancel button to end the cooking, there are two ways you can release the pressure:

Natural-release method. To naturally release the pressure, simply wait until the Instant Pot® has cooled sufficiently for all the pressure to be released and the float valve drops, normally about 10–15 minutes. You can either unplug the Instant Pot® while the pressure releases naturally or let the pressure release while it is still on the Keep Warm function.

Quick-release method. The quick-release method stifles the cooking process and helps unlock the lid for immediate serving. To quickly release the pressure on the Instant Pot®, make sure you are wearing oven mitts, then turn the pressure release handle to the Venting position to let out steam until the float valve drops. This is generally not recommended for starchy items or large volumes of liquid (e.g., soup) so as to avoid any splattering that may occur. Be prepared, because the noise and geyser effect of the releasing steam during the quick-release method can be off-putting. Also, if you own dogs, apparently this release is the most frightening part of the day, so take caution.

Pot-in-Pot Accessories

Pot-in-pot cooking is when you place another cooking dish inside the Instant Pot® for a particular recipe. The Instant Pot® is straightforward and comes with an inner pot and trivet; however, there are many other tricks and recipes that can be made with the purchase of a few other accessories, including a springform pan, cake pan, glass bowl, and ramekins.

7" springform pan. A 7" springform pan is the perfect size for making a cake and many other desserts in an Instant Pot®. It is the right dimension to fit inside the pot, and it makes a dessert for four to six people.

6" cake pan. A 6" pan is excellent for making a small cake in the Instant Pot®. It can serve four to six people depending on the serving size. This pan is perfect for a family craving a small dessert without committing to leftovers.

7-cup glass bowl. This 7-cup bowl fits perfectly in the Instant Pot® and works great for eggs and casseroles that generally would burn on the bottom of the pot insert. The items in the bowl sit up on the inserted trivet and are cooked with the steam and pressure of the pot.

Ramekins. These 4-ounce porcelain individual portions are the perfect vessel for tasty custards.

Steamer basket. The steamer basket helps create a raised shelf for steaming. Shop around, as there are several variations, including metal or silicone steamer baskets. Some even have handles to make it easier to remove them after the cooking process.

Silicone baking cups. The silicone baking cups are great for mini meatloaves, cupcakes, on-the-go frittatas, and little quick breads.

Although these accessories can help you branch out and make different recipes with the Instant Pot®, there are many recipes you can make using just the inner pot and trivet that come with your appliance. These are just handy items you can purchase along the way to use with what will soon become your favorite heat source in the kitchen.

Accessory Removal

Cooking pot-in-pot is a great idea until it's time to remove the inserted cooking dish. Because of the tight space, it is almost impossible to use thick oven mitts to reach down and grip something evenly without tipping one side of the cooking vessel and spilling the cooked item. There are a few ways around this:

Retriever tongs. Retriever tongs are a helpful tool for removing hot bowls and pans from the Instant Pot®.

Mini mitts. Small oven mitts are helpful when lifting pots out of an Instant Pot® after the cooking process, especially the type made of silicone. They are more heat-resistant and less cumbersome than traditional oven mitts, which can prove to be bulky in the tight space of the cooker.

Aluminum foil sling. This is a quick, inexpensive fix to the problem of lifting a heated dish out of an Instant Pot®. Take a 10" × 10" square of aluminum foil and fold it back and forth until you have a 2" × 10" sling. Place this sling underneath the bowl or pan before cooking so that you can easily lift up the heated dish.

Although necessary if you do pot-in-pot cooking, these retrieval tools are not needed if you are simply using the interior pot that comes with the appliance upon purchase. A slotted spoon will do the trick for most other meals.

Cleaning Your Instant Pot®

When cleaning up after using your Instant Pot®, the first thing you should do is unplug it and let it cool down. Then you can break down the following parts to clean and inspect for any trapped food particles:

Inner pot. The inner pot, the cooking vessel, is dishwasher safe; however, the high heat causes rainbowing, or discoloration, on stainless steel. To avoid this, hand wash the pot.

Outer heating unit. Wipe the interior and exterior with a damp cloth. Do not submerge in water, as it is an electrical appliance.

Trivet. The trivet is dishwasher safe or can be cleaned with soap and water.

Lid. The lid needs to be broken down into individual parts before washing. The sealing ring, the float valve, the steam release handle, and the antiblock shield all need to be cleaned in different ways:

- **Sealing ring.** Once this ring is removed, check the integrity of the silicone. If it is torn or cracked, it will not seal properly and may hinder the cooking process, in

which case it should not be used. The sealing ring needs to be removed and washed each time because the ring has a tendency to hold odors when cooking. Vinegar or lemon juice is excellent for reducing odors. You can purchase additional rings for a nominal price. Many Instant Pot® users buy more than one ring and use one for meats and a separate one for desserts and milder dishes.

- **Float valve.** The float valve is a safety feature that serves as a latch lock that prevents the lid from being opened during the cooking process. Make sure that this valve can move easily and is not obstructed by any food particles.

- **Pressure release handle.** This is the venting handle on top of the lid. It can be pulled out for cleaning. It should be loose, so don't worry. This allows it to move when necessary.

- **Antiblock shield.** The antiblock shield is the little silver "basket" underneath the lid. It is located directly below the vent. This shield can and should be removed and cleaned. It blocks any foods, especially starches, so they don't clog the vent.

So, now that you know about all the safety features, buttons, and parts of the Instant Pot® and know how to clean everything, it's time for the fun part. The cooking process is where the excitement begins. From breakfast to dessert and everything in between, The "I Love My Instant Pot®" Paleo Recipe Book has you covered.

2
Breakfast

Fitting breakfast into a busy schedule can seem a bit overwhelming at times, especially if you are following a paleo diet. You will usually have to make your own breakfasts because there really aren't many, if any, paleo-friendly drive-through options. This chapter's got you covered with several to-go meals in addition to sit-down meals made on the fly. The Instant Pot® can help save the day with its shortened cooking time and freedom from having to stand over the skillet. All you have to do is add your ingredients, press a button, and go get ready to tackle your day. Make sure to set aside a prep day during the week so all of your fruits and vegetables are already cut and ready to use.

In addition to the morning-time crunch, most of the breakfast options on the paleo lifestyle seem repetitive. From casseroles to muffins, this chapter offers a wide variety of delicious breakfast recipes, including Bacon Jam, Apple Cinnamon Muffins, and even a Breakfast Casserole with Drop Biscuit Dumplings. And once you get comfortable with some of the basics, you should feel free to get creative and make some of your own morning masterpieces. So, get cooking, and let your family wake up with a new appreciation for their soon-to-be-favorite kitchen gadget!

Champion Breakfast Bowl

Feel like a champion. Work out like a champion. Eat like a champion. After an intense early morning workout on the punching bag, come home to a bowlful of protein to nourish those sore muscles.

- **Hands-On Time: 10 minutes**
- **Cook Time: 9 minutes**

Serves 4

6 large eggs
½ teaspoon sea salt
½ teaspoon freshly ground
   black pepper
2 teaspoons avocado oil
½ cup diced red onion
1 medium red bell pepper,
   seeded and diced
¼ pound ground pork
   sausage
1½ cups water

1   In a medium bowl, whisk together eggs, salt, and pepper. Set aside.

2   Press the Sauté button on the Instant Pot® and heat oil. Stir-fry onion, bell pepper, and sausage 3–4 minutes until sausage starts to brown and onions are tender.

3   Transfer mixture to a lightly greased 7-cup glass bowl. Pour whisked eggs over the sausage mixture.

4   Add water to Instant Pot® and insert trivet. Place dish with egg mixture on trivet. Lock lid. Press the Manual or Pressure Cook button and adjust time to 5 minutes. When timer beeps, quick-release pressure until float valve drops and then unlock lid.

5   Remove dish from pot. Let sit at room temperature 5–10 minutes to allow the eggs to set. Slice and serve.

Sweet Potato Breakfast Bowl

This is a perfect breakfast after an intense morning workout. Let your Instant Pot® be your personal chef and cook this Sweet Potato Breakfast Bowl while you are showering off and getting ready for your day. When ready, ladle a helping of flavor-filled protein and vegetables into your breakfast bowl to help you tackle the day.

- **Hands-On Time: 10 minutes**
- **Cook Time: 10 minutes**

Serves 4

6 large eggs

1 tablespoon Italian seasoning

½ teaspoon sea salt

½ teaspoon freshly ground black pepper

½ pound ground pork sausage

1 large sweet potato, peeled and cubed

1 small yellow onion, peeled and diced

2 cloves garlic, minced

1 medium green bell pepper, seeded and diced

2 cups water

1   In a medium bowl, whisk together eggs, Italian seasoning, salt, and pepper. Set aside.

2   Press the Sauté button on the Instant Pot®. Stir-fry sausage, sweet potato, onion, garlic, and bell pepper 3–5 minutes until onions are translucent.

3   Transfer mixture to a lightly greased 7-cup glass bowl. Pour whisked eggs over the sausage mixture.

4   Add water to the Instant Pot® and insert trivet. Place dish with egg mixture on trivet. Lock lid. Press the Manual or Pressure Cook button and adjust time to 5 minutes. When timer beeps, quick-release pressure until float valve drops and then unlock lid.

5   Remove dish from pot. Let sit at room temperature 5–10 minutes to allow the eggs to set. Slice and serve.

Morning Bacon Parsnips

The runny yolks of a perfectly poached egg are nature's gravy. Don't skip this luxurious step! And if you really want to take this dish to the next level, drizzle some drool-worthy hollandaise over the top.

- **Hands-On Time: 10 minutes**
- **Cook Time: 10 minutes**

Serves 4

1 tablespoon avocado oil

2 slices bacon, diced

1 small yellow onion, peeled and diced

4 cups peeled and diced parsnips

2 tablespoons ghee

3 cloves garlic, minced

1 teaspoon sea salt

½ teaspoon freshly ground black pepper

½ cup water

4 large eggs, poached

1 Press the Sauté button on the Instant Pot® and heat oil. Add bacon and onions. Stir-fry until onions are translucent, 3–5 minutes. Transfer mixture to a lightly greased 7-cup glass bowl. Add parsnips, ghee, garlic, salt, and pepper to bowl and toss to mix.

2 Add water to the Instant Pot® and insert trivet. Place glass dish on top. Lock lid. Press the Manual or Pressure Cook button and adjust time to 5 minutes. When timer beeps, let pressure release naturally until float valve drops and then unlock lid.

3 Remove dish from pot and divide mixture equally among four serving dishes. Garnish each dish with a poached egg.

Apple Cinnamon Muffins

A classic flavor combination, these muffins are a great treat for the family to wake up to as the weather cools. Serve with a slice or two of bacon and a warm cup of tea to round out this wintry breakfast.

- **Hands-On Time: 10 minutes**
- **Cook Time: 9 minutes**

Serves 6

1¼ cups cassava flour
2 teaspoons baking powder
½ teaspoon baking soda
1 teaspoon ground cinnamon
Pinch sea salt
½ teaspoon vanilla extract
3 tablespoons ghee, melted
2 large eggs
⅓ cup pure maple syrup
¼ cup grated red apples
1 cup water

1 In a large bowl, combine flour, baking powder, baking soda, cinnamon, and sea salt.

2 In a medium bowl, combine vanilla, ghee, eggs, syrup, and apples.

3 Pour wet ingredients from the medium bowl into the large bowl with dry ingredients. Gently combine ingredients. Do not overmix. Spoon mixture into 6 lightly greased silicone cupcake liners.

4 Add water to the Instant Pot® and insert trivet or steamer basket. Place cupcake liners on top. Lock lid. Press the Manual or Pressure Cook button and adjust time to 9 minutes. When timer beeps, quick-release pressure until float valve drops and then unlock lid.

5 Remove muffins from pot and set aside to cool 5 minutes.

Blueberry-Orange Muffins

The sweet blueberries and the zesty orange make this the ideal breakfast for mornings on the go.

- **Hands-On Time: 10 minutes**
- **Cook Time: 9 minutes**

Serves 6

1¼ cups cassava flour
2 teaspoons baking powder
½ teaspoon baking soda
Pinch sea salt
½ teaspoon vanilla extract
¼ cup freshly squeezed
    orange juice
1 teaspoon orange zest
3 tablespoons ghee, melted
2 large eggs
⅓ cup pure maple syrup
¼ cup fresh blueberries
1 cup water

1 In a large bowl, combine flour, baking powder, baking soda, and sea salt.

2 In a medium bowl, combine vanilla, orange juice, orange zest, ghee, eggs, and syrup.

3 Pour wet ingredients from the medium bowl into the large bowl with dry ingredients. Gently combine ingredients. Fold in blueberries. Do not overmix. Spoon mixture into 6 lightly greased silicone cupcake liners.

4 Pour water into the Instant Pot® and insert trivet or steamer basket. Place cupcake liners on top. Lock lid. Press the Manual or Pressure Cook button and adjust time to 9 minutes. When timer beeps, quick-release pressure until float valve drops and then unlock lid.

5 Remove muffins from pot and set aside to cool 5 minutes.

Pumpkin Chip Muffins

When everyone else is drinking pumpkin lattes, you can fulfill that urge to splurge with this healthy alternative. The dark chocolate chips provide an element that will make you feel like you are cheating, but the antioxidants will prove otherwise.

- **Hands-On Time: 10 minutes**
- **Cook Time: 9 minutes**

Serves 6

1¼ cups cassava flour
2 teaspoons baking powder
½ teaspoon baking soda
1 teaspoon pumpkin pie spice
Pinch sea salt
¼ cup pumpkin purée
½ teaspoon vanilla extract
1 tablespoon ghee, melted
2 large eggs
⅓ cup pure maple syrup
2 tablespoons dark chocolate chips
1 cup water

1 In a large bowl, combine flour, baking powder, baking soda, pumpkin pie spice, and sea salt.

2 In a medium bowl, combine pumpkin purée, vanilla, ghee, eggs, and syrup.

3 Pour wet ingredients from the medium bowl into the large bowl with dry ingredients. Gently combine ingredients. Fold in dark chocolate chips. Do not overmix. Spoon mixture into 6 lightly greased silicone cupcake liners.

4 Add water to the Instant Pot® and insert trivet or steamer basket. Place cupcake liners on top. Lock lid. Press the Manual or Pressure Cook button and adjust time to 9 minutes. When timer beeps, quick-release pressure until float valve drops and then unlock lid.

5 Remove muffins from pot and set aside to cool 5 minutes.

Sausage Gravy

Whether you serve it with gluten-free biscuits, leftover meatloaf, or morning hash browns, this sausage gravy is the ideal savory addition to your brunch table. And don't forget to go heavy on that black pepper...it's the charm in this Southern breakfast staple.

- **Hands-On Time: 5 minutes**
- **Cook Time: 6 minutes**

Serves 10

2 tablespoons ghee

1 pound ground pork sausage

1 small sweet onion, peeled and diced

¼ cup chicken broth

¼ cup cassava flour

1½ cups unsweetened almond milk

½ teaspoon sea salt

1 tablespoon freshly ground black pepper

WHAT IS CASSAVA FLOUR?

Cassava flour is made from the yucca, a root vegetable that has been dried and ground. Otto's Naturals Cassava Flour is a high-quality cassava flour that is readily available. It is an all-natural, amazing, grain-free replacement for wheat flour and can often be used as a 1:1 substitute in countless recipes. There are no fillers. So, tie up your apron and get to baking!

1 Press the Sauté button on the Instant Pot®. Add ghee and heat until melted. Add sausage and onion; stir-fry 3–5 minutes until onions are translucent. The pork will still be a little pink in places.

2 Add chicken broth to the pot. Lock lid. Press the Manual or Pressure Cook button and adjust time to 1 minute. When timer beeps, quick-release pressure until float valve drops and then unlock lid. Whisk in flour, milk, salt, and pepper.

3 Press the Keep Warm button and let the gravy sit about 5–10 minutes to allow the sauce to thicken. Remove from heat and serve warm.

South-of-the-Border Frittata

This flavorful frittata will have you up and running in the morning. If you are not a fan of cilantro, swap it out with parsley. If a little heat scares your taste buds, substitute the chorizo with breakfast sausage or ground pork, beef, or chicken. Use this recipe as a guide and sub whatever you already have on hand. Frittatas are a great way to clean out the refrigerator.

- **Hands-On Time: 10 minutes**
- **Cook Time: 10 minutes**

Serves 4

4 large whole eggs
4 large egg whites
½ teaspoon sea salt
¼ teaspoon freshly ground black pepper
¼ cup chopped fresh cilantro
2 small Roma tomatoes, seeded and diced
1 medium avocado, peeled and diced
1 tablespoon avocado oil
¼ pound chorizo, loose or cut from casing
1 small red onion, peeled and diced
1 small green bell pepper, seeded and diced
1 cup water

1 In a medium bowl, whisk together eggs, egg whites, salt, and pepper. Add cilantro, tomatoes, and avocado. Set aside.

2 Press the Sauté button on the Instant Pot®. Heat oil and stir-fry chorizo, onion, and green pepper 5 minutes or until chorizo is browned and cooked through. Pat chorizo with paper towels to remove excess oil.

3 Transfer cooked chorizo mixture to a greased 7-cup glass bowl and set aside to cool 5 minutes. Pour whisked eggs over the cooked mixture and stir to combine.

4 Add water to the Instant Pot® and insert trivet. Place dish with egg mixture on trivet. Lock lid. Press the Manual or Pressure Cook button and adjust time to 5 minutes. When timer beeps, let pressure release naturally until float valve drops and then unlock lid.

5 Remove dish from pot and set aside 5–10 minutes to allow the eggs to set. Slice and serve.

Ciao Bella! Egg Muffins

This breakfast is optimal for those mornings spent running around with no time to spare. Whisk yourself away to Italy with these egg muffins made in no time at all. The Instant Pot® makes it easy to get a quick vegetable-filled, protein-packed bite on your way out the door.

- **Hands-On Time: 10 minutes**
- **Cook Time: 15 minutes**

Serves 3

1 tablespoon avocado oil
1 small yellow onion, peeled and diced
4 large eggs
2 teaspoons Italian seasoning
½ teaspoon sea salt
½ teaspoon freshly ground black pepper
1 tablespoon nutritional yeast
4 ounces prosciutto, torn into pieces
1 small Roma tomato, seeded and diced
¼ cup chopped fresh spinach
1 cup water

1 Press the Sauté button on the Instant Pot® and heat oil. Add onion and stir-fry 3–5 minutes until translucent. Transfer onion to a small bowl to cool.

2 In a medium bowl, whisk together eggs, Italian seasoning, salt, pepper, yeast, prosciutto, tomato, and spinach. Stir in cooled onion mixture. Distribute egg mixture evenly among 6 lightly greased silicone cupcake liners.

3 Add water to the Instant Pot® and insert trivet. Place steamer basket on trivet. Carefully place muffin cups on steamer basket. Lock lid. Press Manual or Pressure Cook button and adjust time to 8 minutes. When timer beeps, quick-release pressure until float valve drops and then unlock lid.

4 Remove egg muffins and serve warm.

WHAT ON EARTH IS NUTRITIONAL YEAST?
Nutritional yeast, or nooch as it is affectionately called, is used by a lot of paleo folks and vegans for its cheesy and nutty flavor. It is a deactivated yeast, so it is not the same as baking or brewer's yeast, but it adds another level of richness to many recipes. It can be found in powder or flake form in most specialty grocery stores or online.

Ham and Mushroom Egg Muffins

These make-ahead egg muffins ease the morning rush when you can eat these individual breakfast casseroles on the way to the gym for a little protein boost.

- **Hands-On Time: 10 minutes**
- **Cook Time: 15 minutes**

Serves 3

1 tablespoon avocado oil

½ small yellow onion, peeled and diced

1 cup diced button mushrooms

½ cup small-diced cooked ham

4 large eggs

2 teaspoons yellow mustard

½ teaspoon sea salt

½ teaspoon freshly ground black pepper

1 cup water

1 Press the Sauté button on the Instant Pot® and heat oil. Add onion, mushrooms, and ham; stir-fry 3–5 minutes until onions are translucent. Transfer mixture to a small bowl to cool.

2 In a medium bowl, whisk together eggs, mustard, salt, and pepper. Stir cooled ham mixture into egg mixture. Distribute egg mixture evenly among 6 lightly greased silicone cupcake liners.

3 Add water to the Instant Pot® and insert trivet. Place steamer basket on trivet. Carefully place cupcake liners on steamer basket. Lock lid. Press the Manual or Pressure Cook button and adjust time to 8 minutes. When timer beeps, quick-release pressure until float valve drops and then unlock lid.

4 Remove egg muffins and serve warm.

Bacon, Onion, and Spinach Egg Muffins

Not only are these savory egg muffins a nutritious meal, but you'll avoid a trip to the drive-through window for alternate "food." When purchasing bacon, there are several brands that are paleo-friendly, either from a local farmer, a specialty grocer, or online.

- **Hands-On Time: 10 minutes**
- **Cook Time: 15 minutes**

Serves 3

1 tablespoon avocado oil
½ small yellow onion, peeled and diced
4 slices bacon
1 overflowing cup fresh spinach leaves
4 large eggs
Pinch ground nutmeg
Pinch sea salt
½ teaspoon freshly ground black pepper
1 cup water

1 Press the Sauté button on the Instant Pot® and heat oil. Add onion and bacon; stir-fry 5 minutes until onions are starting to brown and bacon is crisp. Add spinach for 1 minute until wilted. Transfer mixture to a small bowl to cool.

2 In a medium bowl, whisk together eggs, nutmeg, salt, and pepper. Stir cooled onion mixture into egg mixture. Distribute egg mixture evenly among 6 lightly greased silicone cupcake liners.

3 Add water to the Instant Pot® and insert trivet. Place steamer basket on trivet. Carefully place cupcake liners on steamer basket. Lock lid. Press the Manual or Pressure Cook button and adjust time to 8 minutes. When timer beeps, quick-release pressure until float valve drops and then unlock lid.

4 Remove egg muffins and serve warm.

Soft-Boiled Eggs with Steamed Asparagus Dippers

These should just be called *yum*. Eggs cooked in an Instant Pot® are so easy to peel and this dish cooks the asparagus right in the same pot. Crack those eggs open and dip into that glorious soft-boiled yolk. Round out this meal with some prosciutto and melon balls while dining alfresco!

- **Hands-On Time: 5 minutes**
- **Cook Time: 2 minutes**

Serves 4

1 cup water
1 bunch asparagus, woody
  ends removed
4 large eggs

1 Add water to the Instant Pot® and insert steamer basket. Place asparagus on steamer basket and place eggs on top. Press the Manual or Pressure Cook button and adjust time to 2 minutes. When timer beeps, quick-release pressure until float valve drops and then unlock lid.

2 Transfer eggs to an ice bath to stop the cooking process.

3 Place your egg in a soft-boiled egg holder. Hit the side of the egg halfway down around the midway perimeter of the egg. Peel off upper shell. Dig in with a spoon and then dip your asparagus in that glorious yolk.

Bell Pepper Egg Cups

Bell peppers for breakfast? You better believe it! These peppers are stuffed with ground turkey and eggs making this the perfect protein-packed breakfast to start off your day.

- **Hands-On Time: 10 minutes**
- **Cook Time: 15 minutes**

Serves 4

4 large red bell peppers
1 tablespoon avocado oil
½ medium yellow onion, peeled and diced
¾ pound ground turkey
1 small Roma tomato, seeded and diced
1 tablespoon tomato paste
3 large eggs, whisked
1 teaspoon sea salt
1 cup water

1 Cut off the bell pepper tops as close to the tops as possible. Hollow out and discard seeds. Set cleaned peppers aside.

2 Press the Sauté button on the Instant Pot® and heat avocado oil. Add onion and ground turkey. Stir-fry 5 minutes until onions are starting to soften and turkey is browned. Transfer mixture to a medium bowl to cool.

3 Add remaining ingredients except water to the turkey mixture. Stuff equal amounts of mixture into each of the bell peppers.

4 Add water to the Instant Pot® and insert trivet. Set peppers upright on trivet. Lock lid. Press the Manual or Pressure Cook button and adjust time to 10 minutes. When timer beeps, quick release remaining pressure until float valve drops and then unlock lid.

5 Transfer peppers to a platter and serve warm.

Fruity Trail Mix Bowls

If you've missed eating oatmeal on the paleo diet, this recipe is your saving grace. It is warm, filling, and just a good old breakfast comfort meal. The smooth cooked apples and the crunch of the pecans are married together with the warm spices of cinnamon and nutmeg.

- **Hands-On Time: 10 minutes**
- **Cook Time: 5 minutes**

Serves 4

1 (8-ounce) can crushed pineapple, including juice
2 Granny Smith apples, peeled, cored, and diced
¼ cup unsweetened coconut flakes
¼ cup crushed pecans
2 tablespoons raw sunflower seeds
2 tablespoons diced dates
2 tablespoons honey
2 tablespoons cassava flour
½ teaspoon ground cinnamon
¼ teaspoon ground nutmeg
Pinch sea salt
½ cup water

1 Pour crushed pineapple, including juice, into a medium bowl. Add the apples to the pineapple and stir. Add coconut flakes, pecans, sunflower seeds, dates, honey, flour, cinnamon, nutmeg, and salt. Pour ingredients into a lightly greased 7-cup glass bowl.

2 Add water to the Instant Pot® and insert steamer basket. Place the glass bowl on top. Lock lid. Press the Manual or Pressure Cook button and adjust time to 5 minutes. When timer beeps, quick-release pressure until float valve drops and then unlock lid.

3 Spoon into bowls and serve warm.

Mixed Berry Breakfast Syrup

This berrylicious syrup is perfect for your paleo pancakes and gluten-free waffles. Served warm or chilled, this will be a hit at your next brunch or breakfast gathering. Keep refrigerated up to one week if it even lasts that long!

- **Hands-On Time: 5 minutes**
- **Cook Time: 3 minutes**

Yields 1 cup

1 pound frozen mixed berries
1 tablespoon ghee
½ cup pure maple syrup
¼ cup freshly squeezed
     orange juice
1 tablespoon orange zest
Pinch sea salt
1 cinnamon stick

1 Add all ingredients to the Instant Pot®. Lock lid. Press the Manual or Pressure Cook button and adjust time to 3 minutes. When timer beeps, quick-release pressure until float valve drops and then unlock lid.

2 Remove and discard cinnamon stick. Press mixture through a fine-mesh sieve to remove any seeds or skins.

3 Transfer syrup to a lidded container and refrigerate. Serve warm or cold.

Bacon Jam

Sweet and salty, this glorious concoction can give new life to several meals. On top of a burger, alongside your scrambled eggs in the morning, or even licked off a kitchen spoon, Bacon Jam will be your new favorite condiment.

- **Hands-On Time: 10 minutes**
- **Cook Time: 14 minutes**

Yields 2 cups

1 tablespoon coconut oil

1 pound center-cut bacon, diced

1 large yellow onion, peeled and chopped

4 cloves garlic, halved

¼ cup apple cider vinegar

½ cup pure maple syrup

1 chipotle in adobo sauce

1 teaspoon adobo sauce from the chipotle jar

1 teaspoon smoked paprika

1 tablespoon instant espresso powder

½ cup water

1 Press the Sauté button on the Instant Pot® and heat oil. Add bacon and onion; stir-fry 3–4 minutes until bacon fat is rendered and onions are translucent. Add garlic and sauté 1 minute.

2 Discard all but 1 tablespoon bacon grease from pot. Add remaining ingredients. Lock lid. Press the Manual or Pressure Cook button and adjust time to 10 minutes. When timer beeps, quick-release pressure until float valve drops and then unlock lid.

3 Use an immersion blender to blend mixture in pot until preferred consistency is reached. Spoon the jam into a jar and refrigerate up to 2 weeks until ready to use.

Breakfast Casserole with Drop Biscuit Dumplings

Miss that biscuit topping no more. Cassava flour has saved the paleo community. This gluten-free, grain-free, and all-natural product allows a little "breading" back into our lives again. Cooked atop this breakfast casserole, it makes this a complete meal made in no time at all.

- **Hands-On Time: 15 minutes**
- **Cook Time: 8 minutes**

Serves 4

Drop Biscuit Dumplings
½ cup cassava flour
1 teaspoon baking powder
¼ teaspoon baking soda
Pinch sea salt
1 large egg white, whisked
2 tablespoons ghee, melted

Breakfast Casserole
1 pound breakfast pork sausage, loose or cut from casings
½ medium yellow onion, peeled and diced
½ cup diced button or cremini mushrooms
4 large eggs
1 teaspoon freshly ground black pepper

1 In a medium bowl, combine dumpling ingredients. Set aside.

2 Press the Sauté button on the Instant Pot® and stir-fry sausage, onion, and mushrooms 3 minutes to render fat. Transfer mixture to a lightly greased 7-cup glass bowl.

3 Whisk together eggs and black pepper in a small bowl. Pour over sausage mixture.

4 Drop spoonfuls of dumpling mixture over casserole. Place trivet in the Instant Pot® and place the glass bowl on top. Lock lid. Press the Manual or Pressure Cook button and adjust time to 5 minutes. When timer beeps, quick-release pressure until float valve drops and then unlock lid.

5 Remove dish from pot and let cool 5 minutes. Use a paper towel to dab off any additional moisture that may have accumulated on the top of casserole. Serve warm.

Loaded Sweet Potato Hash

Whether you've just finished up a CrossFit class or finally managed to get your kids on the bus, you are starving. This protein-packed power bowl is just what is needed to perk you up and get your body moving for the day.

- **Hands-On Time: 10 minutes**
- **Cook Time: 10 minutes**

Serves 4

6 large eggs

1 tablespoon Italian seasoning

½ teaspoon sea salt

½ teaspoon freshly ground black pepper

½ pound ground pork sausage

1 large sweet potato, peeled and grated

1 small yellow onion, peeled and diced

2 cloves garlic, minced

1 medium green bell pepper, seeded and diced

2 cups water

1 In a medium bowl, whisk together eggs, Italian seasoning, salt, and pepper. Set aside.

2 Press the Sauté button on the Instant Pot®. Stir-fry sausage, sweet potato, onion, garlic, and bell pepper 3–5 minutes until onions are translucent.

3 Transfer mixture to a 7-cup greased glass bowl. Pour whisked eggs over the sausage mixture.

4 Add water to the Instant Pot® and insert trivet. Place dish with egg mixture on trivet. Lock lid. Press Manual or Pressure Cook button and adjust time to 5 minutes. When timer beeps, quick-release pressure until float valve drops and then unlock lid. Remove dish from pot. Let sit at room temperature 5–10 minutes to allow the eggs to set. Slice and serve.

Piggy Tater Bowl with a Poached Egg

This tasty tater bowl is made luxurious with nature's sauce, the beautiful runny yolk of a poached egg! Although white potatoes are not to be consumed every day, this is an all-around treat breakfast especially when you are about to enjoy a full day of hiking with your family or friends.

- **Hands-On Time: 10 minutes**
- **Cook Time: 10 minutes**

Serves 4

1 tablespoon avocado oil

3 slices bacon, diced

1 small yellow onion, peeled and diced

1 small green bell pepper, seeded and diced

4 cups small-diced russet potatoes

2 tablespoons ghee

3 cloves garlic, minced

1 teaspoon sea salt

½ teaspoon freshly ground black pepper

1 cup water

4 large eggs, poached

1 Press the Sauté button on the Instant Pot® and heat oil. Add bacon, onion, green pepper, and potatoes; stir-fry 3–5 minutes until onions are translucent. Transfer mixture to a lightly greased 7-cup glass bowl. Mix in ghee, garlic, salt, and pepper.

2 Add water to the Instant Pot® and insert trivet. Place dish on trivet. Lock lid. Press the Manual or Pressure Cook button and adjust time to 5 minutes. When timer beeps, quick-release pressure until float valve drops and then unlock lid.

3 Remove dish from pot. Spoon mixture into four serving bowls. Garnish each bowl with a poached egg and serve.

Soups, Stews, and Chilis

Soups, stews, and chilis are perfect foods in the paleo world. Most of them utilize the simplest of ingredients: fresh vegetables from the garden and grass-fed meat floating in a sea of beautiful homemade broth. Or at least in the perfect world. Sometimes the ingredients are just quick-grabbed from the store and we make do with what we can find. And that's okay. You are still eating vegetables, meat, and broth.

Or sometimes you may have all the ingredients for a great soup, but you look at the clock and realize you are only an hour out from dinner. Traditionally, you've needed low heat and a long cooking time to marry all the wonderful spices and flavors that make any soup great, but not anymore. The pressurized heat in your Instant Pot® can save the day. Although there is a Slow Cook button on your Instant Pot® for when time isn't an issue, cooking at high pressure can have you serving a finished dinner within an hour. So, break out your ladle because dinner is almost ready. From White Chicken Chili and Mardi Gras Gumbo to Hearty Lamb Stew, this chapter is packed with fresh ideas.

Chicken Broth

Don't skip this recipe after you cook a whole chicken or purchase a cooked rotisserie chicken from the supermarket. Save the carcass and bones to make this nutrient- and mineral-packed Chicken Broth that you can use for a soup base in place of store-bought broth.

- **Hands-On Time: 10 minutes**
- **Cook Time: 30 minutes**

Yields 6 cups

1 chicken carcass from a whole chicken

2 large carrots, peeled and cut into chunks

2 stalks celery, cut into chunks

1 small yellow onion, peeled and chopped

1 bay leaf

2 cloves garlic, halved

½ teaspoon apple cider vinegar

1 teaspoon sea salt

6 cups water

1 Place all ingredients in the Instant Pot®. Press the Manual or Pressure Cook button and adjust time to 30 minutes. When timer beeps, let pressure release naturally until float valve drops and then unlock lid.

2 Use a slotted spoon to remove and discard solids from the broth. Strain the remaining liquid through a fine-mesh sieve or cheesecloth. Refrigerate broth up to 4 days or freeze up to 6 months.

Vegetable Broth

Broths are the base, the very foundation, of almost any soup that you make, so feel free to alter this recipe in order to personalize the flavor of the broth. For example, if you know a guest dislikes garlic, make this broth without it. If you have everything but the parsnip, eliminate it. Tailor this broth to your own taste buds and preferences as well. It will be amazing!

- **Hands-On Time: 10 minutes**
- **Cook Time: 30 minutes**

Yields 6 cups

3 large carrots, peeled and cut into chunks

2 stalks celery, cut into chunks

1 small yellow onion, peeled and chopped

1 medium parsnip, peeled and chopped

1 bay leaf

2 cloves garlic, halved

½ teaspoon apple cider vinegar

1 teaspoon sea salt

6 cups water

1   Place all ingredients in the Instant Pot®. Lock lid. Press the Manual or Pressure Cook button and adjust time to 30 minutes. When timer beeps, let pressure release naturally until float valve drops and then unlock lid.

2   Use a slotted spoon to remove and discard solids from the broth. Strain the remaining liquid through a fine-mesh sieve or cheesecloth. Refrigerate broth up to 4 days or freeze up to 6 months.

Beef Broth

Beef soup bones can be bought at most supermarkets and butcher shops. If they are not on display, don't hesitate to ask. Making your own beef and bone broth is very popular these days, so it won't seem like a weird question. You can also use oxtail or neck bones as a substitute.

- **Hands-On Time: 10 minutes**
- **Cook Time: 30 minutes**

Yields 6 cups

3 pounds beef soup bones

2 large carrots, peeled and cut into chunks

2 stalks celery, cut into chunks

1 small yellow onion, peeled and chopped

1 bay leaf

2 cloves garlic, halved

½ teaspoon apple cider vinegar

1 teaspoon sea salt

6 cups water

1 Place all ingredients in the Instant Pot®. Lock lid. Press the Manual or Pressure Cook button and adjust time to 30 minutes. When timer beeps, let pressure release naturally until float valve drops and then unlock lid.

2 Use a slotted spoon to remove and discard solids from the broth. Strain the remaining liquid through a fine-mesh sieve or cheesecloth. Refrigerate broth up to 4 days or freeze up to 6 months.

To Bean or Not to Bean Chili

Beans are part of the legume family and are not recommended with the paleo lifestyle. Without sounding too scientific, they contain phytates, which lead to improper digestion. They basically inhibit the absorption of certain nutrients and minerals and can lead to a "leaky gut" over time.

- **Hands-On Time: 10 minutes**
- **Cook Time: 40 minutes**

Serves 4

1 tablespoon avocado oil
½ pound ground pork
½ pound ground beef
1 cup diced red onion
1 small green bell pepper, seeded and diced
1 large carrot, peeled and diced
3 cloves garlic, minced
2 tablespoons chili powder
1 teaspoon ground cumin
1 small jalapeño, seeded and diced
1 teaspoon sea salt
1 (28-ounce) can puréed tomatoes, including juice

1 Press the Sauté button on the Instant Pot®. Heat oil. Add the ground pork, ground beef, and onion. Stir-fry 5 minutes until pork is no longer pink.

2 Add remaining ingredients to pot and stir to combine. Lock lid. Press the Meat button and cook for default time of 35 minutes. When timer beeps, let pressure release naturally until float valve drops and then unlock lid. Serve warm.

Chunky Beef Chili

If you're looking to cook up some chili for game day, this recipe is beyond compare. The thinly sliced jalapeños used to top off this hearty bowl of chili will spice up your day and get you through the pregame jitters. Fire up your Instant Pot® and get ready to enjoy some tailgating with your friends.

- **Hands-On Time: 15 minutes**
- **Cook Time: 30 minutes**

Serves 4

1 tablespoon avocado oil

1 pound beef stew cubes

1 medium yellow onion, peeled and diced

4 cloves garlic, minced

1 large carrot, peeled and cut into ½" pieces

2 cups beef broth

2 cups sliced cremini mushrooms

1 tablespoon chili powder

1 tablespoon Italian seasoning

1 teaspoon sea salt

½ teaspoon cayenne pepper

½ teaspoon freshly ground black pepper

2 tablespoons tomato paste

1 (14.5-ounce) can diced tomatoes, including juice

1. Press Sauté button on Instant Pot®. Heat oil and add beef and onion. Stir-fry 3 minutes, searing beef and stir-frying until onions are translucent. Add garlic and carrot; sauté 2 minutes.

2. Add beef broth to pot and deglaze by scraping up any bits from the bottom and sides of the pot.

3. Stir in all remaining ingredients. Lock lid. Press Meat button and cook for default time of 25 minutes. When timer beeps, let pressure release naturally until float valve drops and then unlock lid.

4. Ladle into individual bowls and serve warm.

Hearty Lamb Stew

Forget the family table. Enjoy this incredibly satisfying and hearty stew around the fireplace on a cold winter's night. And, if you happen to have leftovers, it is even better the next day.

- **Hands-On Time: 15 minutes**
- **Cook Time: 40 minutes**

Serves 6

2 tablespoons avocado oil

2 pounds boneless lamb, cubed

1 medium sweet onion, peeled and diced

4 cloves garlic, minced

3 cups beef broth

1 (14.5-ounce) can crushed tomatoes, including juice

2 medium carrots, peeled and diced

1 medium turnip, peeled and small-diced (greens cleaned and chopped)

½ teaspoon fennel seeds

1 teaspoon sea salt

½ teaspoon freshly ground black pepper

¼ cup chopped fresh mint

¼ cup chopped fresh Italian flat-leaf parsley

1 Press the Sauté button on the Instant Pot® and heat oil. Add lamb and onion; stir-fry 3–5 minutes, searing lamb and stir-frying until onions are translucent. Add garlic and sauté 1 minute.

2 Add beef broth and deglaze pot by scraping up any bits from the sides and bottom of the pot. Add tomatoes, including juice, carrots, turnip including chopped greens, fennel seeds, salt, and pepper. Lock lid. Press the Meat button and cook for the default time of 35 minutes. When timer beeps, let pressure release naturally until float valve drops and then unlock lid.

3 Stir in mint. Ladle into individual bowls, garnish with parsley, and serve warm.

Creamy Mushroom Soup

You won't even miss the heavy cream in this dairy-free creamy soup. The puréed cauliflower adds a smoothness and the mushrooms lend earthy and hearty notes needed to make this bowl of soup sing.

- **Hands-On Time: 15 minutes**
- **Cook Time: 25 minutes**

Serves 4

2 tablespoons ghee

1 small sweet onion, peeled and diced

2 cups sliced button mushrooms

1 small head cauliflower, chopped

1 stalk celery, diced

4 cups chicken broth

2 teaspoons dried thyme

1 teaspoon dried oregano

1 teaspoon sea salt

½ teaspoon freshly ground black pepper

MUSHROOM VARIETIES

Mushrooms create a woody and unique flavor to many dishes. Each variety brings a slightly different flavor. Oyster mushrooms have a bit of a briny note, shiitakes have a smoky hint, and morels have a fabulous nuttiness. Change up the variety of mushroom that you use in this recipe or use a mix of varieties for a true "wild mushroom" blend for balance.

1 Press the Sauté button on the Instant Pot® and heat ghee. Add onion and mushrooms; sauté 3–5 minutes until onions are translucent. Transfer half the mushroom mixture to a small bowl and set aside.

2 Add remaining ingredients to the Instant Pot®. Lock lid. Press the Soup button and adjust time to 20 minutes. When timer beeps, let pressure release naturally for 10 minutes. Quick-release any remaining pressure until float valve drops and then unlock lid.

3 Use an immersion blender to blend the soup in the pot until smooth. Stir reserved mushroom mixture into the pot and heat 3–5 minutes.

4 Ladle into bowls and serve warm.

Cream of Broccoli and Bacon Soup

This smooth and creamy broccoli soup is enhanced with the smoky and crunchy bacon garnish. This dish is the perfect comfort meal after a brisk run in the cool fall evenings or even after a family snowball fight in the winter.

- **Hands-On Time: 15 minutes**
- **Cook Time: 30 minutes**

Serves 4

1 teaspoon ghee
6 pieces of bacon, diced
1 medium sweet onion, peeled and diced
1 large carrot, peeled and diced
2 stalks celery, diced
1 pound broccoli, chopped
1 tablespoon nutritional yeast
1 teaspoon sea salt
1 teaspoon freshly ground black pepper
4 cups chicken broth

1 Press the Sauté button on the Instant Pot® and heat the ghee. Add half the bacon and heat 3–5 minutes until crispy. Set aside on a plate lined with paper towels to cool. Add remaining bacon and onion; sauté 3–5 minutes until the onions are translucent.

2 Add all remaining ingredients to Instant Pot®. Lock lid. Press the Soup button and adjust time to 20 minutes. When timer beeps, quick-release any remaining pressure until float valve drops and then unlock lid.

3 Use an immersion blender to blend the soup in the pot until smooth.

4 Ladle the soup into serving bowls and garnish with reserved bacon. Serve warm.

Tom Kha Goong

Adding the shrimp at the end of the cooking process keeps it from getting overcooked. The other ingredients, however, go through the steaming process to really marry all the rich flavors—so much so that you'll think that this soup has been slow cooking for hours.

- **Hands-On Time: 15 minutes**
- **Cook Time: 25 minutes**

Serves 4

1 tablespoon coconut oil
6 green onions, sliced
1 cup sliced shiitake mushrooms
2 cloves garlic, minced
3 cups vegetable broth
1 tablespoon Thai red curry paste
1 tablespoon fish sauce
2 tablespoons minced lemongrass (soft inner layer only)
1 teaspoon honey
1 cup canned coconut milk
1 tablespoon fresh lime juice
¼ teaspoon dried red pepper flakes
1 teaspoon sea salt
½ teaspoon white pepper
¼ cup chopped fresh cilantro
1 pound medium shrimp, peeled and deveined

1 Press the Sauté button on the Instant Pot® and heat oil. Add green onions and mushrooms; sauté 3–5 minutes until mushrooms are tender. Add garlic and sauté 1 minute.

2 Add remaining ingredients except shrimp to pot. Lock lid. Press the Soup button and adjust time to 15 minutes. When timer beeps, quick-release pressure until float valve drops and then unlock lid.

3 Add shrimp and simmer 5 minutes until opaque and pink.

4 Ladle into bowls and serve warm.

Kentucky Derby Burgoo

Burgoo? What's that? It's a traditional stew in Louisville especially celebrated during the week of the Kentucky Derby. Once cooked in large iron kettles, this concoction used meat from that day's hunting expedition and vegetables that were already in the house. Burgoo typically isn't ever made the same way twice and is different from family to family, so let this recipe be your guide and tweak it as you see fit.

- **Hands-On Time: 15 minutes**
- **Cook Time: 40 minutes**

Serves 6

2 tablespoons avocado oil

½ pound chicken thighs, cubed

½ pound beef, cubed

4 cups beef broth

1 stalk celery, diced

1 cup asparagus, trimmed and cut into 1" pieces

½ cup sliced fresh or frozen okra

2 small red potatoes, peeled and cubed

1 small carrot, peeled and diced

1 small yellow onion, peeled and diced

4 cloves garlic, minced

1 (15-ounce) can crushed tomatoes, including juice

2 tablespoons Worcestershire sauce

1 teaspoon sea salt

1 teaspoon freshly ground black pepper

1 Press the Sauté button on the Instant Pot®. Heat the oil and add the chicken and beef cubes. Sear meat 3–4 minutes until browned on all sides.

2 Add broth and deglaze the pot by scraping up bits from the sides and bottom of the pot.

3 Add remaining ingredients. Lock lid. Press the Meat button and cook for the default time of 35 minutes. When timer beeps, let pressure release naturally until float valve drops and then unlock lid.

4 Ladle into individual bowls and serve warm.

White Chicken Chili

This warmth-inducing, crowd-pleasing dish will have your friends asking if they can watch the game at your house every weekend. And not only will you have the winning dish of the day, but you will actually get to visit with your guests instead of being stuck in the kitchen cooking. Let your Instant Pot® do all the work!

- **Hands-On Time: 10 minutes**
- **Cook Time: 20 minutes**

Serves 4

1 tablespoon avocado oil

1 pound ground chicken

1 medium yellow onion, peeled and diced

1 stalk celery, diced

3 cloves garlic, minced

1 (28-ounce) can diced tomatoes, including liquid

1 (4-ounce) can diced green chilies, including liquid

1 teaspoon sea salt

1 tablespoon chili powder

1 tablespoon fresh thyme leaves

1 Press the Sauté button on the Instant Pot® and heat oil. Add chicken, onion, and celery; stir-fry 5 minutes or until chicken is no longer pink. Add garlic and sauté 1 minute.

2 Stir in remaining ingredients. Lock lid. Press the Manual or Pressure Cook button and adjust time to 15 minutes. When timer beeps, let pressure release naturally until float valve drops and then unlock lid.

3 Ladle into individual bowls and serve warm.

Savory Acorn Squash Soup

Acorn squash has an inherently sweet taste, but coupled with some savory pantry spices and salty bacon, this squash takes on a new life.

- **Hands-On Time: 10 minutes**
- **Cook Time: 23 minutes**

Serves 4

½ cup water

2 medium acorn squash, halved and seeds removed

1 tablespoon ghee

2 slices bacon, diced

1 small yellow onion, peeled and diced

1 stalk celery, diced

1 medium carrot, peeled and diced small

3 cloves garlic, quartered

3 cups chicken broth

1 cup canned coconut milk

1 teaspoon celery seed

1 teaspoon sea salt

1 teaspoon freshly ground black pepper

⅛ teaspoon cayenne pepper

1 Add water to the Instant Pot® and insert trivet. Place squash on trivet. Lock lid. Press the Manual or Pressure Cook button and adjust time to 4 minutes. When timer beeps, quick-release pressure until float valve drops and then unlock lid.

2 Transfer squash to a cutting board and discard liquid from pot. When cool enough to work with, scoop out squash meat and set aside. Discard skin.

3 Press the Sauté button on the Instant Pot® and heat ghee until melted. Add bacon, onion, celery, and carrot; stir-fry 3–4 minutes until fat is rendered from bacon and onion is translucent. Add garlic and sauté 1 minute.

4 Add chicken broth and deglaze pot by scraping up the bits from the bottom and sides of the pot. Add all remaining ingredients and lock lid. Press the Soup button and adjust time to 15 minutes. When timer beeps, quick-release pressure until float valve drops and then unlock lid.

5 Use an immersion blender to purée the soup in the pot, or use a blender and purée it in batches.

6 Ladle the soup into bowls and serve warm.

Chicken Taco Soup

This soup is filled with chicken, vegetables, and taco spices. The chicken is cooked in its juices and even pulled apart directly in the pot to ensure the tenderness and moistness of the meat.

- **Hands-On Time: 15 minutes**
- **Cook Time: 25 minutes**

Serves 4

1 tablespoon avocado oil

1 small red onion, peeled and diced

1 medium yellow bell pepper, seeded and diced

3 cloves garlic, quartered

1 (28-ounce) can diced tomatoes, including juice

1 cup water

½ pound boneless, skinless chicken breasts

1 medium jalapeño, seeded and diced

1 (2.25-ounce) can diced black olives, drained

2 tablespoons chili powder

1 tablespoon ground cumin

1 teaspoon sea salt

1 teaspoon freshly ground black pepper

½ cup chopped fresh cilantro, divided

1 medium avocado, pitted, peeled, and sliced

1 Press the Sauté button on the Instant Pot® and heat oil. Add onion and bell pepper; sauté 3–5 minutes until onions are translucent. Add garlic and heat an additional minute. Add tomatoes, including juice, and water; deglaze pot by scraping up any bits from the bottom and sides of the pot.

2 Add chicken, jalapeño, black olives, chili powder, cumin, salt, pepper, and ¼ cup cilantro. Lock lid. Press the Manual or Pressure Cook button and adjust time to 15 minutes. When timer beeps, quick-release pressure until float valve drops and then unlock lid. Use two forks to shred the chicken in the pot. Let simmer 5 minutes.

3 Ladle soup into bowls and garnish with avocado slices and remaining cilantro.

Creamy Tomato Basil Soup

Skip the usual step of peeling the tomatoes for this recipe. Once steamed and blended, there will be no trace of the skins. Also, if you can get your hands on some heirloom tomatoes, try them in this dish. They are the ugly duckling of the produce world, but their swan wings will be revealed once you take a slurp of this creamy soup.

- **Hands-On Time: 10 minutes**
- **Cook Time: 15 minutes**

Serves 4

1 tablespoon coconut oil

1 small sweet onion, peeled and diced

1 stalk celery, thinly sliced

8 medium tomatoes, seeded and quartered

3 cups chicken broth

¼ cup julienned fresh basil, divided

1 teaspoon sea salt

1 teaspoon freshly ground black pepper

1 cup unsweetened almond milk

1. Press the Sauté button on the Instant Pot® and heat oil. Add onion and celery; sauté 3–5 minutes until onions are translucent. Add tomatoes and sauté 3 minutes or until tomatoes start to break down.

2. Add broth, ⅛ cup basil, salt, and pepper to pot. Lock lid. Press the Manual or Pressure Cook button and adjust time to 7 minutes. When timer beeps, quick-release pressure until float valve drops and then unlock lid.

3. Add almond milk. Use an immersion blender to purée the soup in the pot or purée it in a stand blender in batches.

4. Ladle into bowls and garnish with remaining basil. Serve warm.

COMPANION PLANTS FOR GARDEN TOMATOES

Just like grapes meant for fine wines take on some of the flavors of the plants grown around them, so do tomatoes. Not only do dill and basil plants add another level of flavor to a gardener's tomato plants, but they also help repel disease and destructive insects harmful to the tomato plants.

Mardi Gras Gumbo

Because the booze usually flies freely during Mardi Gras, make sure you get some solid food in your stomach before you get started. So plug in your Instant Pot® and get your taste buds ready to take a quick vacation down South. This dish is traditionally served over rice, but this gumbo is just as delicious as is or over some riced cauliflower.

- **Hands-On Time: 15 minutes**
- **Cook Time: 25 minutes**

Serves 6

1 tablespoon ghee

1 medium yellow onion, peeled and diced

2 stalks celery, diced

1 small red bell pepper, seeded and diced

½ pound skinless, boneless chicken thighs, cut into ½" pieces

1 pound andouille sausage, sliced

3 cloves garlic, minced

3 cups chicken broth

1 teaspoon Worcestershire sauce

¼ cup cassava flour

1 pound medium shrimp, peeled, deveined, tails removed

1 tablespoon gumbo filé powder

1 teaspoon garlic powder

1 teaspoon cayenne pepper

1 teaspoon fresh thyme leaves

¼ cup chopped fresh Italian flat-leaf parsley, divided

10-ounces frozen or fresh sliced okra

1 (14.5-ounce) can stewed tomatoes, including juice

1 Press the Sauté button on the Instant Pot® and heat ghee. Add onion, celery, and bell pepper; sauté 3–5 minutes until onions are translucent. Add chicken, sausage, and garlic; stir-fry 2–3 minutes until chicken is no longer pink.

2 Add chicken broth and deglaze the pot by scraping up the brown bits from the bottom and sides of the pot. Add Worcestershire sauce, flour, shrimp, filé powder, garlic powder, cayenne pepper, thyme, ⅛ cup parsley, okra, and tomatoes. Lock lid. Press the Soup button and adjust time to 15 minutes. When timer beeps, let pressure release naturally for 5 minutes. Quick-release any remaining pressure until float valve drops and then unlock lid.

3 Ladle gumbo into bowls and garnish with remaining parsley.

Quick Vegetable Soup

This low-calorie vegetable soup is loaded with nutrients, and it is a great starter soup for a family that generally isn't crazy about vegetables. Add chicken or sausage to make this a more complete meal.

- **Hands-On Time: 15 minutes**
- **Cook Time: 10 minutes**

Serves 4

4 cups vegetable broth

2 stalks celery, diced

1 small carrot, peeled and diced

1 small yellow onion, peeled and diced

2 cloves garlic, minced

1 (15-ounce) can diced tomatoes, including juice

1 medium turnip, peeled and diced

1 medium zucchini, diced

1 tablespoon Italian seasoning

1 teaspoon sea salt

1 teaspoon freshly ground black pepper

1 Add all ingredients to the Instant Pot®. Lock lid. Press the Manual or Pressure Cook button and adjust time to 10 minutes. When timer beeps, quick-release pressure until float valve drops and then unlock lid.

2 Ladle into individual bowls and serve warm.

Hamburger Soup

Skip the processed foods, trans fats, and wasted money of drive-through meals. This Hamburger Soup hits all the flavors of your favorite burger. And don't skip that pickle garnish—it makes the soup!

- **Hands-On Time: 10 minutes**
- **Cook Time: 15 minutes**

Serves 4

1 tablespoon avocado oil

1 pound ground beef

1 medium yellow onion, peeled and diced

1 medium green bell pepper, seeded and diced

1 (15-ounce) can diced tomatoes, including juice

2 teaspoons yellow mustard

1 teaspoon smoked paprika

1 teaspoon garlic powder

½ teaspoon sea salt

4 cups beef broth

2 cups shredded iceberg lettuce

½ cup diced dill pickles

1 Press the Sauté button on the Instant Pot® and heat oil. Add beef, onion, and green pepper; sauté 3–5 minutes until beef begins to brown.

2 Add tomatoes, including juice, mustard, paprika, garlic powder, salt, and beef broth to pot. Lock lid. Press the Manual or Pressure Cook button and adjust time to 7 minutes. When timer beeps, quick-release pressure until float valve drops and then unlock lid.

3 Stir in lettuce and simmer 3 minutes. Ladle into bowls and garnish with diced dill pickles. Serve warm.

Oma's Sausage and Cabbage Soup

If you're craving a home-cooked hearty meal, become your own German grandma. The simplicity and heartiness of the meal will taste like you've been making it for years. Nothing soothes the soul better than a warm bowl of soup.

- **Hands-On Time: 10 minutes**
- **Cook Time: 13 minutes**

Serves 4

1 tablespoon avocado oil

2 medium leeks, diced (white and light green portions only)

1 stalk celery, diced

1 (16-ounce) bag coleslaw mix

8 ounces precooked sausage links, sliced on an angle

1 medium turnip, peeled and diced

1 tablespoon German stone-ground mustard

2 tablespoons fresh thyme leaves, divided

½ teaspoon caraway seeds

½ teaspoon sea salt

½ teaspoon freshly ground black pepper

4 cups beef broth

1. Press the Sauté button on the Instant Pot® and heat oil. Add leeks and celery; sauté 3–5 minutes until onion is tender.

2. Add remaining ingredients to pot and lock lid. Press the Manual or Pressure Cook button and adjust time to 8 minutes. When timer beeps, quick-release pressure until float valve drops and then unlock lid.

3. Ladle soup into bowls and serve warm.

Creamy Ham and Root Veggie Soup

A meal straight from the farm. What a perfect soup to make from a hodgepodge of vegetables from your CSA box that you're not sure what to do with. This bowl of comfort is a great introduction to some root vegetables that you might not have cooked with before.

- **Hands-On Time: 15 minutes**
- **Cook Time: 20 minutes**

Serves 4

3 tablespoons ghee

1 medium sweet onion, peeled and diced

3 cloves garlic, minced

1 large carrot, peeled and diced

1 cup peeled and cubed celeriac

1 small rutabaga, peeled and diced

4 cups chicken broth

1 teaspoon sea salt

1 teaspoon freshly ground black pepper

2 tablespoons fresh thyme leaves, divided

1 tablespoon cooking sherry

2 cups cubed cooked ham

1 Press the Sauté button on the Instant Pot® and heat ghee. Add onion and sauté 3–5 minutes until translucent. Add garlic and sauté 1 minute until fragrant.

2 Add carrot, celeriac, rutabaga, chicken broth, salt, pepper, and 1 tablespoon thyme to pot and lock lid. Press the Manual or Pressure Cook button and adjust time to 10 minutes. When timer beeps, quick-release pressure until float valve drops and then unlock lid.

3 Use an immersion blender to purée the soup in the pot or purée in a stand blender in batches. Stir in sherry and ham and let simmer 5 minutes.

4 Ladle into bowls and garnish with remaining thyme. Serve warm.

WHAT IS A CSA?

CSA stands for community-supported agriculture. It allows a local community member to receive a box per week or biweekly made up of a produce collection from regional farmers. You are essentially buying a share of the crop which is paid for upfront allowing the farmers to plan better for their season while you receive crops that are completely fresh and haven't left a large carbon footprint in its wake.

Curried Carrot Soup

Fresh and creamy, this Curried Carrot Soup is a perfect lunch companion to a big green salad.

- **Hands-On Time: 10 minutes**
- **Cook Time: 14 minutes**

Serves 4

2 tablespoons ghee

3 cups peeled and sliced carrots

6 green onions, sliced, greens and whites separated

3 cups chicken broth

1 cup canned coconut milk

1 tablespoon curry powder

½ teaspoon ground cumin

¼ teaspoon ground ginger

1 teaspoon sea salt

1 teaspoon freshly ground black pepper

1 medium lime, quartered

1 Press the Sauté button on the Instant Pot® and melt ghee. Add carrots and onion whites; stir-fry 3–4 minutes until onions are tender.

2 Add all remaining ingredients except onion greens and lime to pot and lock lid. Press the Manual or Pressure Cook button and adjust time to 10 minutes. When timer beeps, quick-release pressure until float valve drops and then unlock lid.

3 Use an immersion blender to purée the soup in the pot or purée in a stand blender in batches.

4 Ladle into bowls and garnish with onion greens. Serve warm with a squeeze of lime.

4

Appetizers and Sauces

Living within certain diet requirements is never harder than when you are with a group of friends. Chips and dips and cheesy everything seem to swarm the tables. But boring plates of inedible food doesn't have to be your fate. Bring a healthy paleo option to share. Or, better yet, throw your own party and show the folks what they've been missing! Appetizers are a great way to bring a group of people together to enjoy a game or hold them over until you serve a meal.

But you don't want to have to wear your chef hat all day, stuck in the kitchen, so let the Instant Pot® be your helpful sous chef. Quick, hot food in minutes? Now that's how you throw a party! With amazing appetizers ranging from Broccoli-Zucchini Hummus and Liver Pâté to Tandoori-Style Chicken Wings and Deviled Eggs, the only problem you'll have incorporating the recipes in this chapter into your next social event will be deciding which ones to make. And after the appetizers have been devoured, make some of the rich sauces from this chapter such as Bolognese or Puttanesca to ladle over some spiralized zucchini or carrots. Your guests will leave full and satisfied not even knowing that they ate "paleo" all night!

Deviled Eggs

The hardest part about making this recipe is usually the actual peeling of the eggs—but not with the Instant Pot®. It produces the most peelable eggs, so you won't have all those pesky gouges in the sides. Note that the cooking time will vary slightly depending on the size of the eggs as well as how fresh they are.

- **Hands-On Time: 15 minutes**
- **Cook Time: 4 minutes**

Yields 12 deviled eggs

1 cup water
6 large eggs
3 tablespoons mayonnaise
1 teaspoon yellow mustard
½ teaspoon dill pickle juice
2 teaspoons finely diced dill pickles
⅛ teaspoon sea salt
⅛ teaspoon freshly ground black pepper
Smoked paprika, for garnish

1 Add water to the Instant Pot® and insert steamer basket. Place eggs on basket. Press the Manual or Pressure Cook button and adjust time to 4 minutes. When timer beeps, quick-release pressure until float valve drops and then unlock lid. Transfer eggs to an ice bath to stop the cooking process.

2 Peel eggs. Slice each egg in half lengthwise and place yolks in a small bowl. Place egg white halves on a serving tray.

3 Add mayonnaise, mustard, pickle juice, diced pickles, salt, and pepper to the bowl with the yolks. Use a fork to blend until smooth.

4 Spoon or pipe the yolk filling into the egg white halves. Sprinkle with paprika for garnish.

Mini Chili Polpette

Polpette literally means "meatballs" and there are many versions across the various regions of Italy. With these Mini Chili Polpette you can introduce your guests to a new word and wow their taste buds at the same time. And, they will be even more impressed when you show them how easy it is to cook this dish in your Instant Pot®.

- **Hands-On Time: 10 minutes**
- **Cook Time: 7 minutes**

Yields 24 meatballs

1 pound ground beef

1 large egg

¼ cup chopped fresh Italian flat-leaf parsley

¼ cup almond meal

2 tablespoons finely chopped green onions

1 tablespoon chili powder

1 tablespoon Dijon mustard

1 teaspoon sea salt

2 tablespoons avocado oil, divided

½ cup water

1 In a medium bowl, combine ground beef, egg, parsley, almond meal, green onions, chili powder, mustard, and salt. Form the mixture into 24 meatballs.

2 Press the Sauté button on the Instant Pot® and heat 1 tablespoon oil. Add half the meatballs to the pot and sear about 3 minutes, turning them to brown all sides. Remove the first batch and set aside. Add the remaining oil and repeat with the remaining meatballs. Remove the meatballs from the pan.

3 Add water to the Instant Pot® and insert steamer basket. Place the meatballs evenly on the steamer basket. Lock lid. Press the Manual or Pressure Cook button and adjust time to 1 minute. When timer beeps, quick-release pressure until float valve drops and then unlock lid.

4 Transfer the polpette to a serving tray and serve warm.

"Cheesy" Spinach Crab Dip

The nutritional yeast gives this dip a cheesy flavor that your guests won't even know is missing. For a browned top, place the dip under the broiler 1–3 minutes until it browns to your desired doneness. Serve with a variety of fresh vegetables such as radishes, broccoli florets, cauliflower, squash rounds, celery, and carrots.

- **Hands-On Time: 10 minutes**
- **Cook Time: 16 minutes**

Serves 8

2 tablespoons ghee
1 small sweet onion, peeled and diced
1 cup diced zucchini
1 overflowing cup fresh spinach leaves
½ teaspoon sea salt
¾ pound lump crab meat
2 tablespoons nutritional yeast
½ teaspoon Worcestershire sauce
2 teaspoons prepared horseradish
1 teaspoon Old Bay Seasoning
1 teaspoon sriracha
2 teaspoons lemon zest
¼ teaspoon freshly ground black pepper
2 cups water

1 Press the Sauté button on the Instant Pot® and heat ghee. Add onion and zucchini. Stir-fry 3–5 minutes until zucchini is tender. Add spinach and heat 1 additional minute to wilt spinach.

2 Transfer sautéed ingredients and salt to a food processor or blender and pulse until smooth.

3 Combine zucchini purée and remaining ingredients except water in a medium bowl until well blended. Spoon into a lightly greased 7-cup glass bowl.

4 Add water to the Instant Pot® and insert trivet. Place glass bowl on trivet. Lock lid. Press the Manual or Pressure Cook button and adjust time to 10 minutes. When timer beeps, quick-release pressure until float valve drops and then unlock lid.

5 Remove dish and serve warm.

Endive Boats with Chicken Salad

Talk about time-saving—the chicken and the egg are cooked together. Make sure your chicken isn't cut too small or it will dry out. Twenty-five endive leaves are suggested in this recipe, but if you have leftover chicken salad, it is perfect served the next day as a lettuce wrap for a quick lunch!

- **Hands-On Time: 15 minutes**
- **Cook Time: 5 minutes**

Yields 3 cups

1 pound chicken breasts, cut into 1" cubes

1½ cups water

1 large egg

½ teaspoon sea salt

¼ teaspoon freshly ground black pepper

1 stalk celery, finely diced

1 teaspoon yellow mustard

½ teaspoon dill pickle juice

1 tablespoon finely diced dill pickle

½ cup mayonnaise

2 slices bacon, cooked and crumbled

25 endive leaves

1 Add chicken and water to the Instant Pot®. Add steamer basket to pot and place egg on top. Lock lid. Press the Manual or Pressure Cook button and adjust time to 5 minutes. When timer beeps, quick-release pressure until float valve drops and then unlock lid.

2 Transfer egg to an ice bath to stop the cooking process.

3 Use a slotted spoon to transfer the chicken to a cutting board. When cool enough to work with, finely chop the chicken. Add to a medium bowl. Peel egg and dice. Add to bowl.

4 Add salt, pepper, celery, mustard, pickle juice, pickles, mayonnaise, and bacon. Stir ingredients until well combined. Refrigerate covered until ready to serve.

5 Spoon chicken salad onto endive leaves. Serve.

IS MAYONNAISE PALEO?

Homemade mayonnaise is your best bet to stay strictly paleo of course. It is quick to make and you can control the ingredients that go into your recipe. Primal Kitchen makes a glorious jarred regular mayonnaise as well as an avocado mayonnaise that can be found online or in specialty stores. *Pssst:* don't forget to try their Chipotle Lime Mayo too!

Tandoori-Style Chicken Wings

This recipe still captures the flavors and essence of tandoori-style without the dairy. Perfect "dude" food, these are a sophisticated twist on the traditional buffalo-style staple found at most tailgating parties.

- **Hands-On Time: 10 minutes**
- **Cook Time: 10 minutes**

Serves 6

1 small yellow onion, peeled and diced

2" piece ginger, peeled and minced

4 cloves garlic, minced

2 tablespoons fresh lime juice

1 cup canned coconut milk

2 tablespoons avocado oil

1 tablespoon ground cumin

1 tablespoon ground coriander

2 teaspoons sea salt

1 teaspoon white pepper

1 teaspoon cayenne pepper

2 tablespoons tomato paste

3 pounds chicken wings, separated at the joint if necessary

1 cup chicken broth

¼ cup chopped fresh mint

1 In a large bowl, combine onion, ginger, garlic, lime juice, coconut milk, avocado oil, cumin, coriander, salt, white pepper, cayenne pepper, and tomato paste. Add wings to mixture and toss. Refrigerate covered at least 1 hour or up to overnight.

2 Add chicken broth to the Instant Pot® and insert steamer basket. Add chicken wings, arranging them so they aren't sitting on top of one another; place them standing up if necessary. Lock lid. Press the Manual or Pressure Cook button and adjust time to 10 minutes. When timer beeps, let pressure release naturally for 5 minutes. Quick-release any remaining pressure until float valve drops and then unlock lid. Use a slotted spoon to transfer the wings to a serving tray. Garnish with chopped mint and serve.

3 Optional: Before garnishing, place the wings on a baking sheet and broil 3 minutes on each side to crisp up the chicken.

THE THICK LAYER IN A CAN OF COCONUT MILK
Don't throw away that can of coconut milk if you notice a thick layer on top and a cloudy thinner liquid underneath. This is normal. The top layer is the coconut cream, which is full of the natural fats and flavor. Use this first. Also, if you have a warm kitchen, try putting the can of coconut milk in the refrigerator up to an hour before using to ensure this layer. On a yummy note, for desserts, whip up this thick layer with a little honey for some dairy-free whipped cream.

Sesame-Orange Chicken Wings

The brightness of the orange, the sweetness of the maple syrup, the saltiness of the coconut aminos, and the bit of heat from the ginger and red pepper flakes makes these wings a balanced and delicious addition to your appetizer spread for your family and guests.

- **Hands-On Time: 10 minutes**
- **Cook Time: 16 minutes**

Serves 6

¼ cup freshly squeezed orange juice

2 tablespoons orange zest

¼ cup pure maple syrup

2 tablespoons coconut aminos

2" piece ginger, peeled and minced

3 cloves garlic, minced

2 tablespoons sesame oil

½ teaspoon dried red pepper flakes

1 teaspoon sea salt

1 tablespoon arrowroot flour

1 bunch green onions, sliced and separated into whites and greens

3 pounds chicken wings, separated at the joint if necessary

1 cup chicken broth

¼ cup toasted sesame seeds

1 In a large bowl, combine orange juice, orange zest, syrup, coconut aminos, ginger, garlic, sesame oil, red pepper flakes, salt, flour, and whites of green onions. Transfer 2 tablespoons of the sauce to a small bowl and set aside.

2 Add wings to sauce in large bowl and toss. Refrigerate covered at least 1 hour or up to overnight.

3 Add chicken broth to the Instant Pot® and insert steamer basket. Add chicken wings, arranging them so they aren't sitting on top of one another; place them standing up if necessary. Lock lid. Press the Manual or Pressure Cook button and adjust time to 10 minutes. When timer beeps, let pressure release naturally for 5 minutes. Quick-release any remaining pressure until float valve drops and then unlock lid.

4 Use a slotted spoon to transfer the wings to a baking sheet. Brush with the 2 tablespoons of reserved sauce. Broil 3 minutes on each side to add some crisp to the chicken.

5 Transfer to a serving tray and garnish with sesame seeds and the greens of the onions.

WHAT ARE COCONUT AMINOS?
A gluten-free and soy-free alternative to soy sauce, this underrated condiment is a staple in paleo diets. Used 1:1 and an incredible taste substitute, this sauce is created from aged coconut sap and sea salt. Coconut aminos are found in most specialty grocers as well as online.

Broccoli-Zucchini Hummus

A perfect dip served with crudités and some fresh pita slices for your non-paleo guests. Though hummus is traditionally made with chickpeas, this Broccoli-Zucchini Hummus offers not only a handful of nutrients, but a flavor combination that is out of this world.

- **Hands-On Time: 15 minutes**
- **Cook Time: 2 minutes**

Serves 10

1 cup water
1 small head broccoli, diced
1 medium zucchini, large chopped
½ cup tahini
4 cloves garlic, quartered
2 tablespoons fresh lemon juice
1 teaspoon lemon zest
½ teaspoon ground cumin
½ teaspoon smoked paprika
½ teaspoon sea salt
¼ teaspoon freshly ground black pepper
¼ cup extra-virgin olive oil, plus extra for garnish
2 tablespoons finely diced jarred roasted red peppers

1 Add water to the Instant Pot® and insert steamer basket. Add broccoli and zucchini. Lock lid. Press the Manual or Pressure Cook button and adjust time to 2 minutes. When timer beeps, quick-release pressure until float valve drops and then unlock lid.

2 Transfer broccoli and zucchini to a food processor or blender and pulse 2–3 times. Add tahini, garlic, lemon juice, lemon zest, cumin, paprika, salt, and pepper; pulse 5–6 times. Add olive oil 1 tablespoon at a time, pulsing between additions, until desired consistency is reached. Transfer to a serving dish.

3 Garnish with diced roasted red peppers placed in a small circle in the center. Add an extra drizzle of olive oil. Serve.

Burgundy Mushrooms

These Burgundy Mushrooms are a side dish you'll find yourself making again and again. Don't skip the bacon in this recipe as the meatiness and saltiness add a deep flavor to this insanely rich and earthy side dish. Serve alongside a grilled steak and you'll have a meal to be proud of.

- **Hands-On Time: 5 minutes**
- **Cook Time: 30 minutes**

Serves 8

½ cup ghee

3 cloves garlic, halved

16 ounces whole button mushrooms

16 ounces whole baby bella mushrooms

1½ cups dry red wine

1 teaspoon Worcestershire sauce

1 teaspoon dried thyme

1 tablespoon Dijon mustard

1 teaspoon ground celery seed

½ teaspoon freshly ground black pepper

3 cups beef broth

2 slices bacon

1 Press the Sauté button on the Instant Pot®. Add ghee and melt. Add garlic and mushrooms and toss to coat with ghee. Stir-fry 3 minutes until mushrooms soften.

2 Add red wine. Press the Sauté button and adjust temperature to Less; simmer 5 minutes.

3 Add remaining ingredients to the pot. Lock lid. Press the Manual button and adjust time to 20 minutes. When timer beeps, let pressure release naturally until float valve drops and then unlock lid. Discard bacon and garlic.

4 Use a slotted spoon to transfer mushrooms to a serving bowl. Serve warm.

Mushrooms Stuffed with Sausage and Kimchi

If you are true paleo, you probably have a jar of kimchi in the back of your refrigerator. So, if you are in a pinch for a quick appetizer, this recipe is for you. The kimchi and its acidity blends nicely with the breakfast sausage. If cilantro repels you, substitute some Italian seasoning or dried basil; both work beautifully and add a slightly different flavor note to this dish.

- **Hands-On Time: 10 minutes**
- **Cook Time: 8 minutes**

Yields 10–12 mushrooms

1 tablespoon avocado oil

¼ pound ground breakfast sausage

2 tablespoons finely minced yellow onion

1 tablespoon diced drained kimchi

2 tablespoons mayonnaise

1 teaspoon dried cilantro

8 ounces whole baby bella mushrooms (about 10–12), stemmed

1 cup water

2 tablespoons chopped fresh Italian flat-leaf parsley

1 Press the Sauté button on the Instant Pot® and heat oil. Add sausage and onion; stir-fry 5–6 minutes until sausage is no longer pink. Transfer mixture to a small bowl and use paper towels to dab off excess oil and fat. Add kimchi, mayonnaise, and cilantro.

2 Stuff an equal amount of mixture into each mushroom cap and place on the steamer basket. Pour water into the Instant Pot®. Insert steamer basket and lock lid. Press the Manual or Pressure Cook button and adjust time to 2 minutes. Adjust pressure to Low. When timer beeps, quick-release pressure until float valve drops and then unlock lid.

3 Transfer mushrooms to a serving plate. Garnish with chopped parsley. Serve warm.

WHAT TO DO WITH MUSHROOM STEMS?

Don't throw away those mushroom stems. Clean and dice them, and place in a lidded container and refrigerate. These stems, which are usually discarded, are ideal additions to breakfast scrambles, sauces, and even to green smoothies in the morning.

Steamed Shrimp with Cocktail Sauce

This is one of the easiest and most-appreciated appetizers. It is a low-calorie alternative to those rich chip and dips that are always present at a group get-together.

- **Hands-On Time: 10 minutes**
- **Cook Time: 0 minutes**

Serves 8

Cocktail Sauce

½ cup paleo ketchup

2 tablespoons prepared horseradish

1 teaspoon fresh lemon juice

¼ teaspoon Worcestershire sauce

¼ teaspoon sriracha sauce

Steamed Shrimp

1 cup water

2 pounds large shrimp, peeled and deveined (tails on)

1 Combine cocktail sauce ingredients until well blended. Refrigerate lidded until ready to use.

2 Add water to the Instant Pot® and insert steamer basket. Place shrimp on the steamer basket. Lock lid. Press the Steam button and adjust time to 0 minutes. When timer beeps, quick-release pressure until float valve drops and then unlock lid.

3 Serve shrimp, warm or cold, with cocktail sauce.

ALL KETCHUP IS NOT CREATED EQUAL

Most commercial ketchups are filled with sugars; however, you have options. There are many sugar-free homemade recipes online. Also, you can find several premade and paleo-approved options at specialty stores and online.

Liver Pâté

Luxury...pure luxury. And for such a decadent dish, it is really quite simple to make, especially with your Instant Pot®. Served with crudités or even with some bread toasts for your non-paleo guests, this spread is sure to delight your friends.

- **Hands-On Time: 15 minutes**
- **Cook Time: 9 minutes**

Yields 1½ cups

2 tablespoons ghee
1 pound chicken livers
1 piece bacon, diced
1 large shallot, peeled and diced
2 cloves garlic, minced
¼ cup cabernet
2 tablespoons water
1 bay leaf
1 large egg
1 teaspoon capers, rinsed
2 tablespoons cooking sherry
Pinch ground nutmeg
2 tablespoons melted ghee

1 Press the Sauté button on the Instant Pot® and heat 2 tablespoons ghee. Add chicken livers, bacon, and shallot. Sauté 3 minutes or until chicken livers are lightly browned on all sides and shallot is tender. Add garlic and stir-fry 1 minute.

2 Add wine and water and scrape up any bits from the bottom and sides of the pot. Add bay leaf and place egg on top. Lock lid. Press the Manual or Pressure Cook button and adjust time to 5 minutes. When timer beeps, quick-release pressure until float valve drops and then unlock lid. Discard bay leaf.

3 Transfer egg to a water bath to stop the cooking process. Peel egg and dice.

4 Transfer egg and remaining ingredients to a food processor or blender. Pulse ingredients until smooth.

5 Transfer mixture to a large lidded container and refrigerate until ready to serve. Serve chilled.

Steamed Artichokes with Lemon-Herb Butter

Not only are artichokes a fun food to eat with other people, but also they are an absolute superfood packed with phytonutrients and anti-inflammatory properties that help protect against cancer, heart disease, and diabetes just to name a few ailments. In addition, they help detoxify your liver.

- **Hands-On Time: 10 minutes**
- **Cook Time: 5 minutes**

Serves 6

6 medium artichokes
1 cup water
3 cloves garlic, quartered
Juice of 1 medium lemon
1 teaspoon sea salt

LEMON-HERB BUTTER DIPPING SAUCE

The following Lemon-Herb Butter Dipping Sauce is a delicious dipping sauce to accompany the light nature of the steamed artichoke. To make this recipe, in a small bowl combine ¼ cup melted ghee, 2 cloves minced garlic, ½ teaspoon herbes de Provence (or Italian seasoning), 1 tablespoon fresh lemon juice, and a pinch of sea salt and freshly ground black pepper.

1 Clean the artichokes by clipping off the top third of the leaves and removing the tougher exterior leaves. Trim the bottoms so that they have a flat surface to prop up in the Instant Pot®.

2 Add water, garlic, and lemon juice to the Instant Pot® and insert trivet. Place artichokes upright in a steamer basket and lower onto the trivet. Sprinkle artichokes with salt. Lock lid. Press the Manual or Pressure Cook button and adjust time to 5 minutes. When timer beeps, quick-release pressure until float valve drops and then unlock lid.

3 Transfer the artichokes to a plate, and serve warm.

Rutabaga Fries with Rosemary Dipping Sauce

Traditional baked rutabaga fries can take 45 minutes up to an hour to bake. In the meantime, all the moisture is sucked out. By steaming the fries and then broiling them, the fries result in a crispy outside and a beautifully steamed and tender inside. Couple that with this flavorful rosemary dip, and your taste buds will be in heaven.

- **Hands-On Time: 10 minutes**
- **Cook Time: 13 minutes**

Serves 8

Rosemary Dipping Sauce
½ cup mayonnaise
1 tablespoon finely chopped fresh rosemary
½ teaspoon lemon juice
½ teaspoon lemon zest
¼ teaspoon sea salt
⅛ teaspoon cayenne pepper

Rutabaga Fries
1 large rutabaga, peeled, trimmed, and cut into ½" sticks
2 tablespoons avocado oil
1 teaspoon sea salt, or more to taste
½ teaspoon freshly ground black pepper
½ teaspoon garlic powder
1 cup water

1 Line a large baking sheet with parchment paper. Set oven to broil.

2 Combine Rosemary Dipping Sauce ingredients in a small bowl. Refrigerate covered until ready to use.

3 Place rutabaga in a medium bowl and toss with avocado oil, salt, pepper, and garlic powder.

4 Pour water into the Instant Pot® and insert steamer basket. Add fries to steamer basket. Lock lid. Press the Steam button and adjust time to 3 minutes. When timer beeps, quick-release pressure until float valve drops and then unlock lid.

5 Transfer fries to the prepared baking sheet and scatter evenly. Broil 10 minutes or until crisp and browned, tossing once halfway through cooking. Season with additional salt if desired. Serve warm with chilled dipping sauce.

Broccoli-Cauli Sausage Tots

Choosing different types of sausage will alter the flavor of these tots as the broccoli and cauliflower take on the flavors of whatever they are combined with. These crispy and savory tots will disappear off the plate in minutes!

- **Hands-On Time: 15 minutes**
- **Cook Time: 37 minutes**

Yields 20 tots

1 cup water
2 cups fresh broccoli florets
2 cups fresh cauliflower florets
1 shallot, finely minced
¼ pound mild Italian sausage
1 large egg
1 teaspoon dried oregano
½ teaspoon sea salt

1 Add water to the Instant Pot® and insert steamer basket. Add broccoli and cauliflower. Lock lid. Press the Manual or Pressure Cook button, and adjust time to 2 minutes. When timer beeps, quick-release pressure until float valve drops and then unlock lid.

2 Preheat oven to 400°F. Line a baking sheet with parchment paper.

3 Transfer broccoli and cauliflower to a food processor or blender. Pulse 5–6 times until smooth. Transfer to a medium bowl.

4 Add shallot, sausage, egg, oregano, and salt. Combine until well mixed. Form into 20 tots and place on the prepared baking sheet. Bake 35 minutes. Serve warm.

Salsa Verde

Tomatillos are the star of this green sauce, or "salsa verde." It is terrific served with chicken enchiladas, fish taco wraps, Salsa Verde Pulled Pork (see Chapter 8), and many other dishes.

- **Hands-On Time: 5 minutes**
- **Cook Time: 2 minutes**

Serves 8

1 pound tomatillos, outer husks removed and halved

2 small jalapeños, seeded and chopped

1 small onion, peeled and diced

½ cup chopped fresh cilantro

1 teaspoon ground coriander

2 teaspoons sea salt

1½ cups water

1 Place tomatillos in the Instant Pot®. Add enough water to cover the tomatillos. Lock lid. Press the Manual or Pressure Cook button, and adjust timer to 2 minutes. When timer beeps, let pressure release naturally until float valve drops and then unlock lid. Drain pot.

2 Add tomatillos, jalapeños, onion, cilantro, coriander, sea salt, and 1½ cups water to a food processor or blender. Pulse until well combined, about 1–2 minutes.

3 Transfer to a serving dish, cover, and chill in the refrigerator before serving.

Bolognese Sauce

Rich and meaty, Bolognese originated in Bologna, Italy; however, its power has won the world's heart. Make a jar of this on food prep day and enjoy the tasty sauce during the week served over spiraled zucchini, carrots, or whatever your heart likes to zoodle!

- **Hands-On Time: 15 minutes**
- **Cook Time: 20 minutes**

Yields 6 cups

2 tablespoons ghee

2 stalks celery, finely diced

1 medium carrot, peeled and finely diced

½ medium Vidalia onion, peeled and finely diced

4 cloves garlic, quartered

1 pound ground Italian sausage

2 slices bacon, diced

1 (28-ounce) can crushed tomatoes, including juice

½ cup beef broth

2 tablespoons chopped fresh basil

2 tablespoons fresh thyme leaves

1 teaspoon sea salt

½ teaspoon freshly ground black pepper

½ cup unsweetened almond milk

1 Press the Sauté button on the Instant Pot® and heat ghee. Add celery, carrot, and onion; sauté 2–3 minutes until onions are tender. Add garlic, Italian sausage, and bacon; stir-fry 3–5 minutes until sausage is no longer pink. Drain off and discard any excess fat.

2 Stir in tomatoes, including juice, and scrape up the bits from the sides and bottom of the pot. Add broth, basil, thyme, salt, and pepper. Lock lid. Press the Manual or Pressure Cook button and adjust time to 10 minutes. When timer beeps, let pressure release naturally for 5 minutes. Quick-release any remaining pressure until float valve drops and then unlock lid. Stir in almond milk.

3 Simmer unlidded 2–3 minutes. Pour sauce into a lidded container or jar and refrigerate until ready to use. Use within 5 days.

HOW TO MAKE HOMEMADE ALMOND MILK
Soak 1 cup unsalted raw almonds covered in water for at least 24 hours. Rinse and drain. In a stand blender or food processor, pulse 1¾ cups water and almonds. Strain liquid through a fine-mesh sieve or cheesecloth. Refrigerate up to 2–3 days.

Marinara Sauce

One of the tastiest and most versatile sauces out there, Marinara Sauce is a great one to keep on hand. You can add it to zoodled vegetables, to a bowl of meatballs, to a skillet of ground beef with added vegetables—and the list goes on.

- **Hands-On Time: 10 minutes**
- **Cook Time: 10 minutes**

Yields 4 cups

1 (28-ounce) can crushed tomatoes, including juice

1 stalk celery, finely diced

1 medium carrot, peeled and finely diced

½ medium red onion, peeled and finely diced

4 cloves garlic, quartered

2 tablespoons chopped fresh basil

2 tablespoons chopped fresh Italian flat-leaf parsley

1 tablespoon fresh thyme leaves

1 teaspoon sea salt

½ teaspoon freshly ground black pepper

½ cup beef broth

1 Combine all ingredients in the Instant Pot®. Lock lid. Press the Manual or Pressure Cook button and adjust time to 10 minutes. When timer beeps, let pressure release naturally for 5 minutes. Quick-release any remaining pressure until float valve drops and then unlock lid.

2 Use an immersion blender to blend the sauce in the pot until smooth.

3 Pour the sauce into a lidded container or jar and refrigerate until ready to use. Use within 5 days.

Puttanesca Sauce

No need to add salt to this dish because the olives, anchovies, and capers hit this beautiful note in the recipe. *Puttanesca* literally translates to "in the style of the prostitutes," because the intriguing aroma of the sauce was how the prostitutes from Naples, Italy, would lure customers to their door.

- **Hands-On Time: 5 minutes**
- **Cook Time: 10 minutes**

Yields 5 cups

2 tablespoons avocado oil

1 small red onion, peeled, halved, and cut into half-moons

4 large cloves garlic, minced

1 (28-ounce) can diced tomatoes, including juice

¼ cup Kalamata olives, pitted and diced

¼ cup green olives, pitted and diced

4 anchovy fillets, finely chopped or smashed with the back of a fork

2 tablespoons drained capers

2 teaspoons dried oregano

½ teaspoon dried red pepper flakes

½ cup chicken broth

2 tablespoons chopped fresh Italian flat-leaf parsley

1 Combine all ingredients in the Instant Pot®. Lock lid. Press the Manual or Pressure Cook button and adjust time to 10 minutes. When timer beeps, let pressure release naturally for 5 minutes. Quick-release any remaining pressure until float valve drops and then unlock lid.

2 Pour sauce into a lidded container or jar and refrigerate until ready to use. Use within 5 days.

Tomato Curry Sauce

This creamy dairy-free sauce is excellent served over cauliflower "rice," seafood, or chicken.

- **Hands-On Time: 10 minutes**
- **Cook Time: 10 minutes**

Yields 4 cups

1 (28-ounce) can crushed tomatoes, including juice
½ medium onion, peeled and finely diced
4 cloves garlic, quartered
1 tablespoon minced fresh ginger
½ teaspoon garam masala
½ teaspoon turmeric powder
¼ teaspoon red pepper flakes
¼ teaspoon ground cinnamon
1 tablespoon fresh thyme leaves
1 teaspoon sea salt
½ teaspoon freshly ground black pepper
½ cup canned coconut milk

1 Combine all ingredients in the Instant Pot®. Lock lid. Press the Manual or Pressure Cook button and adjust time to 10 minutes. When timer beeps, let pressure release naturally for 5 minutes. Quick-release any remaining pressure until float valve drops and then unlock lid.

2 Use an immersion blender to blend the sauce in the pot until smooth.

3 Pour sauce into a lidded container or jar and refrigerate until ready to use. Use within 5 days.

5

Side Dishes

Sometimes in our attempt to live a paleo life, we cook up a chicken breast or steak and then fall short on the extras. All the while our gorgeous farmers' market and CSA (community-supported agriculture) produce takes a backseat in the refrigerator and gets a little slimy. Unfortunately, sometimes those nutrient-rich vegetables never make it to our plates. Not only is it a waste of healthful food, but it is also a big waste of money. With the Instant Pot®, you can have flavorful seasonal vegetables in minutes while the main dish is being prepared. Also, cooking vegetables in your Instant Pot® retains more nutrients than boiling them on the stovetop or roasting them in the oven. So, while you're grilling that steak outdoors in the summer or charring some chicken on an indoor grilling pan, why not take a few extra minutes to round out the meal? With recipes such as Lemon Ghee Broccoli and Honey-Glazed Carrots to Southern Squash Casserole and Bacon-Apple Brussels Sprouts, you will be happy you took the few extra moments to prepare a side dish. And your body will thank you!

Nutty Holiday Sweet Potatoes

Happy holidays to you and your family! Sweet potatoes are a traditional staple on most winter celebration tables and this dish is no exception. You won't miss the marshmallows and ooey-gooey recipes of the past. These sweet potatoes will quench all of your comfort memories.

- **Hands-On Time: 10 minutes**
- **Cook Time: 10 minutes**

Serves 6

2½ pounds sweet potatoes, peeled and diced large

2 cups water

1 tablespoon minced fresh ginger

½ teaspoon sea salt

1 tablespoon pure maple syrup

1 tablespoon ghee

¼ cup unsweetened almond milk

2 tablespoons crushed walnuts

1   Add potatoes and water to the Instant Pot®. Lock lid. Press the Manual or Pressure Cook button and adjust time to 10 minutes. When timer beeps, let pressure release naturally until float valve drops and then unlock lid.

2   Drain water from pot. Add ginger, salt, syrup, ghee, and milk (1 tablespoon at a time) to the potatoes. Use an immersion blender or masher to cream the potatoes to desired consistency. Stir in walnuts. Serve warm.

PEELING FRESH GINGER

Fresh ginger can seem difficult to navigate with its uneven surface and all the branches. Instead of taking your fingers' safety into the war zone, simply take the edge of a spoon and scrape the peel off of a fresh gingerroot before you grate or mince it.

Honey-Glazed Carrots

We all dress up during the holidays, so why not give the simple carrot a makeover? By adding a little honey and ghee, these beta-carotene cargo trains come to life and deliver a flavorful punch for your guests or family any time of the year.

- **Hands-On Time: 5 minutes**
- **Cook Time: 5 minutes**

Serves 4

1 pound carrots, peeled and diced large

¼ cup freshly squeezed orange juice

½ cup water

1 tablespoon ghee

2 tablespoons honey

½ teaspoon sea salt

---

1 Add carrots, orange juice, and water to the Instant Pot®. Lock lid. Press the Manual or Pressure Cook button and adjust time to 5 minutes. When timer beeps, quick-release pressure until float valve drops and then unlock lid.

2 Use a slotted spoon to transfer the carrots to a bowl. Toss with ghee, honey, and salt. Serve warm.

MEASURING HONEY WITHOUT THE MESS

When measuring sticky liquids like honey, maple syrup, or molasses, warm up the measuring cup or spoon by rinsing it first with hot water. Your liquid won't stick to your cup, making cleanup much easier and the measurement more accurate!

Bacon-Apple Brussels Sprouts

The saltiness of the bacon and the sweetness of the apple help counter the bitter flavor that some may detect in Brussels sprouts. Rounded out even more with the earthiness of the onions and the citrus kick from the zest, this dish will have your family asking for seconds!

- **Hands-On Time: 5 minutes**
- **Cook Time: 8 minutes**

Serves 4

1 tablespoon avocado oil

2 slices bacon, diced

1 cup water

1 pound Brussels sprouts, trimmed and halved

2 medium Granny Smith apples, peeled, cored, and diced

1 small sweet onion, peeled and sliced

½ teaspoon sea salt

2 teaspoons orange zest

1 Press the Sauté button on the Instant Pot® and heat oil. Add bacon and stir-fry 3–5 minutes or until almost crisp and the fat is rendered. Add water and deglaze the pot by scraping the bits from the sides and bottom of the pot.

2 Add Brussels sprouts, apples, and onion. Lock lid. Press the Manual button and adjust time to 3 minutes. When timer beeps, quick-release pressure until float valve drops and then unlock lid.

3 Transfer the Brussels sprouts to a serving dish. Garnish with salt and orange zest. Serve warm.

Mixed Southern Greens

This recipe calls for turnip and collard greens, but you can swap or add kale, mustard greens, chard, or whatever your heart desires. For the fat, this recipe calls for bacon, but you can swap out a ham hock or turkey neck. That is part of the greatness of Southern cooking. Recipes are merely a suggestion.

- **Hands-On Time: 10 minutes**
- **Cook Time: 10 minutes**

Serves 6

1 bunch turnips with greens
1 bunch collard greens, chopped (ribs removed)
1 small Vidalia onion, peeled and diced
¼ cup apple cider vinegar
1 teaspoon sriracha
2 slices bacon
1 cup chicken broth
1 teaspoon honey
½ teaspoon sea salt
¼ teaspoon freshly ground black pepper

1 Remove spines from turnip greens and discard. Chop leaves. Rinse turnips. Peel and dice.

2 Place all ingredients in the Instant Pot®. Lock lid. Press the Manual or Pressure Cook button and adjust time to 10 minutes. When timer beeps, let pressure release naturally until float valve drops and then unlock lid. Discard bacon.

3 Transfer the greens and turnips to a dish and serve warm.

Dilled Purple Potatoes

Wait! Potatoes? Yes, that's right. Potatoes are now considered paleo in small quantities. Opinions do change. But here's the rub. If nightshades are your enemy or you are trying to drop a few pounds, this starchy tuber needs to stay underground. However, if your family is craving a little comfort, go for it. It is a natural product but just cook it as a savory treat from time to time and not so much in regular rotation.

- **Hands-On Time: 5 minutes**
- **Cook Time: 10 minutes**

Serves 6

1½ **pounds baby purple potatoes**
4 **tablespoons ghee, divided**
2 **cloves garlic, minced**
3 **tablespoons chopped dill, divided**
2 **cups water**
1 **teaspoon sea salt**

1 Use a fork to pierce each potato 3 or 4 times. Press the Sauté button on the Instant Pot®. Heat 2 tablespoons ghee and add potatoes, garlic, and 1 tablespoon dill; sauté 3 minutes, stirring frequently.

2 Add water to the pot. Lock lid. Press the Manual or Pressure Cook button and adjust time to 7 minutes. When timer beeps, quick-release pressure until float valve drops and then unlock lid.

3 Use a slotted spoon to transfer the potatoes to a serving bowl. Toss with remaining ghee, dill, and salt. Serve.

Lemon Ghee Broccoli

Simply divine. Broccoli is such a healthy and inexpensive side that goes with just about any protein. The lemon lends a freshness and the ghee gives it that little bit of fat to help our taste buds along. Because heads of broccoli vary in size, season sparingly and taste as you go before adding more salt.

- **Hands-On Time: 5 minutes**
- **Cook Time: 2 minutes**

Serves 2

½ **cup water**
Juice of ½ medium lemon
1 **head broccoli, chopped into bite-sized pieces**
2 **tablespoons ghee**
½ **teaspoon sea salt**

1 Add water and lemon juice to the Instant Pot® and insert steamer basket. Add broccoli. Lock lid. Press the Manual or Pressure Cook button, and adjust time to 2 minutes. When timer beeps, quick-release pressure until float valve drops and then unlock lid.

2 Transfer broccoli to a serving bowl. Add ghee and salt. Toss to mix. Serve immediately.

Herbed Fingerling Potatoes and Onions

Fingerling potatoes are stubby little counterparts to the mighty russet, but that size can work to the favor of the busy home chef. There is no need to peel or dice these small tubers. Give them a good scrub and they are ready for steamed perfection in the Instant Pot®.

- **Hands-On Time: 5 minutes**
- **Cook Time: 9 minutes**

Serves 6

1½ pounds fingerling potatoes (unpeeled)

4 tablespoons ghee, divided

1 small yellow onion, peeled, halved, and sliced into half-moons

2 cloves garlic, chopped

2 sprigs rosemary

2 cups water

1 teaspoon sea salt

1 tablespoon fresh thyme leaves

1 Use a fork to pierce each potato 2 or 3 times. Press the Sauté button on the Instant Pot®. Heat 2 tablespoons ghee and add potatoes, onion, garlic, and rosemary. Stir-fry 3 minutes or until onions are translucent.

2 Add water to the pot. Lock lid. Press the Manual or Pressure Cook button and adjust time to 6 minutes. When timer beeps, quick-release pressure until float valve drops and then unlock lid.

3 Use a slotted spoon to transfer potatoes and onions to a serving bowl. Discard rosemary. Toss with remaining ghee, salt, and thyme. Serve.

DRIED HERBS IN A PINCH

If you're in a hurry and out of fresh herbs, use some Italian seasoning from your spice drawer. Add 2 teaspoons to the Instant Pot® while cooking and then use another 2 teaspoons to garnish the finished product. When garnishing, pinch the dried herbs between your fingers to release some of the oil from the leaves. This adds another dimension of flavor to your dish.

Kohlrabi, Kale, and Karrots

Balanced in flavors and exploding with nutrients, this kindred trio is a knockout that teams nicely with a tender chicken or savory steak dish.

- **Hands-On Time: 10 minutes**
- **Cook Time: 12 minutes**

Serves 6

2 teaspoons apple cider vinegar

1 tablespoon pure maple syrup

½ teaspoon sea salt

Pinch cayenne pepper

Pinch ground nutmeg

1 bunch kale

2 tablespoons ghee

1 large kohlrabi, peeled and diced

3 medium carrots, peeled and sliced

3 cloves garlic, quartered

1 cup water

1   In a small bowl, whisk together vinegar, syrup, salt, cayenne pepper, and nutmeg. Set aside.

2   Remove spines from the middle of the kale leaves and discard. Chop kale.

3   Press the Sauté button on the Instant Pot®. Heat ghee and add kohlrabi and carrots. Stir-fry 3–4 minutes until vegetables start to get tender. Add garlic quarters and heat 1 additional minute.

4   Add water to the pot. Lock lid. Press the Manual or Pressure Cook button and adjust time to 5 minutes. When timer beeps, let pressure release naturally for 5 minutes. Quick-release any remaining pressure until float valve drops and then unlock lid.

5   Stir in kale and simmer 1–2 minutes until it wilts.

6   Use a slotted spoon to transfer the pot ingredients to a serving dish. Add vinegar mixture and toss to mix. Serve warm.

Steamed Beets

Keep the skin on these beets to reap the benefits of the fiber. Plus, peeling them just gets messy. Adding this root vegetable to your meal rotation is a smart move. They contain betalains, which provide anti-inflammatory and detoxification support. Also, mix it up by trying golden beets as well. They can be prepared in the same way.

- **Hands-On Time: 10 minutes**
- **Cook Time: 10 minutes**

Serves 6

1 cup water
6 medium beets, trimmed
    and quartered
Juice of ½ medium orange
2 teaspoons chopped fresh dill
1 teaspoon sea salt

1 Add water to the Instant Pot® and insert steamer basket. Place beets in basket. Lock lid. Press the Manual or Pressure Cook button and adjust time for 10 minutes. When timer beeps, quick-release pressure until float valve drops and then unlock lid.

2 Transfer beets to a bowl. Add orange juice, dill, and salt. Toss and serve warm.

Purple Cauliflower

Purple Cauliflower is just so pretty, but this recipe works with orange and white cauliflower too. To take this dish from florets to cauliflower rice, just drain the water after cooking. Add the olive oil back to the pot. Press the Sauté button and use a potato masher to mash the cauliflower directly in the pot. Season with salt and pepper. Voila!

- **Hands-On Time: 5 minutes**
- **Cook Time: 2 minutes**

Serves 4

1 medium head cauliflower,
    cut into florets
1 cup water
Drizzle of extra-virgin olive oil
Pinch sea salt
Pinch freshly ground black
    pepper

1 Add water to the Instant Pot® and insert steamer basket. Add cauliflower. Lock lid. Press the Steam button and adjust time for 2 minutes. When timer beeps, quick-release pressure until float valve drops and then unlock lid.

2 Transfer cauliflower to a serving bowl. Garnish with olive oil, salt, and pepper. Serve warm.

German Red Potatoes

Not only does the Instant Pot® make this German classic quick to fix, but also there is no need to take the extra time to peel the potatoes. The color of the red potatoes not only adds to the optics of the dish, but the skins also provide most of the fiber, vitamins, and minerals found in the potato.

- **Hands-On Time: 5 minutes**
- **Cook Time: 16 minutes**

Serves 4

2 tablespoons apple cider vinegar
1 teaspoon honey
1 teaspoon sea salt
1 teaspoon freshly ground black pepper
¼ teaspoon caraway seeds
8 small red potatoes, diced (unpeeled)
2 slices bacon, diced
1 small yellow onion, peeled and diced
2 cloves garlic, minced
1 cup water
2 tablespoons chopped fresh Italian flat-leaf parsley

1 In a small bowl, whisk together vinegar, honey, salt, pepper, and caraway seeds. Set aside.

2 Use a fork to pierce each potato 3 or 4 times. Press the Sauté button on the Instant Pot® and add bacon. Cook bacon until crisp, about 5–8 minutes. Transfer bacon to a plate lined with paper towels.

3 Add potatoes and onion to bacon grease in the pot. Stir-fry 3–4 minutes until onions are translucent. Add garlic and sauté 1 minute.

4 Add water to pot. Lock lid. Press the Manual or Pressure Cook button and adjust time to 3 minutes. When timer beeps, quick-release pressure until float valve drops and then unlock lid.

5 Use a slotted spoon to transfer potatoes and onions to a serving bowl. Toss with bacon and vinegar mixture. Garnish with parsley. Serve.

Eggplant-Olive Ratatouille

The somewhat plain-flavored eggplant and zucchini take on the incredible Mediterranean flavors of the basil and garlic of this dish. The olives lend a salty and almost fantastic bitter flavor to round out this side dish that is exquisite served with a grilled steak or tender chicken breast.

- **Hands-On Time: 10 minutes**
- **Cook Time: 7 minutes**

Serves 4

1 tablespoon coconut oil

1 medium sweet onion, peeled and diced

1 small yellow bell pepper, seeded and diced

1 large eggplant, peeled and diced into 1" cubes

3 cloves garlic, minced

1 (28-ounce) can diced tomatoes, including juice

¼ cup sliced green olives

1 medium zucchini, diced into 1" cubes

1 teaspoon sea salt

½ teaspoon freshly ground black pepper

¼ cup chopped fresh basil

2 tablespoons chopped fresh Italian flat-leaf parsley

1 Press the Sauté button on the Instant Pot® and heat coconut oil. Add onion and bell pepper; stir-fry 3–4 minutes until onions are translucent. Add eggplant and garlic; toss and cook 1 minute.

2 Add diced tomatoes including juice and scrape sides and bottom of pot. Add olives, zucchini, salt, pepper, and basil. Lock lid. Press the Manual or Pressure Cook button and adjust time to 2 minutes. When timer beeps, quick-release pressure until float valve drops and then unlock lid.

3 Use a slotted spoon to transfer ingredients to a large bowl. Garnish with parsley. Serve warm.

Southern Squash Casserole

Void of the milk and bread or crackers that are in most squash casserole recipes, this version will thrill even the harshest of critics. Most home gardeners are overwhelmed during the year with an overhaul of summer squash and this is a great go-to recipe for the win.

- **Hands-On Time: 15 minutes**
- **Cook Time: 5 minutes**

Serves 6

2 cups water, divided

2 large yellow squash, diced

1 small Vidalia onion, peeled and diced

4 large eggs, whisked

¼ cup almond meal

2 tablespoons ghee, melted

2 teaspoons nutritional yeast

½ teaspoon sea salt

½ teaspoon freshly ground black pepper

1 Pour 1 cup water into the Instant Pot® and insert steamer basket. Place squash and onion in basket. Lock lid. Press the Manual or Pressure Cook button and set time to 0 minutes. Adjust pressure to Low. When timer beeps, quick-release pressure until float valve drops and then unlock lid.

2 Transfer squash to a medium bowl. Let cool 5 minutes. Discard liquid from the pot.

3 Add eggs, almond meal, ghee, yeast, salt, and pepper to a medium bowl. Transfer to greased 7-cup glass bowl.

4 Add 1 cup water to the Instant Pot®. Insert steamer basket or trivet. Place the squash dish in pot. Lock lid. Press the Manual or Pressure Cook button and adjust time to 5 minutes. When timer beeps, quick-release pressure until float valve drops and then unlock lid.

5 Remove squash casserole. Let rest 5 minutes. Use a paper towel to dab off any additional moisture. Serve warm.

Broccoli Casserole

Broccoli casserole is found on the table at most Southern get-togethers, and it is traditionally cooked with condensed mushroom soup, cheese, and a butter cracker layer. The condensed soup is replaced with the slurry made from almond milk and cassava flour, which is added to the sautéed mushroom mixture. The nutritional yeast adds a little cheese flavor, and the ghee and almond meal sub for the "cracker" layer. But really, the broccoli is the star.

- **Hands-On Time: 15 minutes**
- **Cook Time: 14 minutes**

Serves 6

¾ cup unsweetened almond milk

2 tablespoons cassava flour

1 tablespoon ghee

½ cup chopped yellow onion

1 cup diced button or cremini mushrooms

4 cups chopped fresh broccoli

4 large eggs

1 teaspoon nutritional yeast

½ teaspoon sea salt

½ teaspoon freshly ground black pepper

¼ cup almond meal

1 cup water

1 In a small bowl, create a slurry by whisking together almond milk and flour. Set aside.

2 Lightly grease a 7-cup glass bowl. Set aside.

3 Press the Sauté button and adjust temperature to Less. Heat ghee. Add onion, mushrooms, and broccoli; stir-fry 4–5 minutes until onions are translucent. Add slurry and mix together 1 minute until thickened.

4 Crack eggs in a medium bowl. Quickly whisk in a spoonful of the mixture from the pot to temper the eggs. Add yeast, salt, and pepper. Add remaining pot mixture and stir until combined. Transfer mixture to the prepared dish. Sprinkle almond meal in an even layer over casserole.

5 Add water to the Instant Pot® and insert steamer basket. Insert dish and lock lid. Press the Manual or Pressure Cook button and adjust time to 8 minutes. When timer beeps, quick-release pressure until float valve drops and then unlock lid.

6 Remove broccoli casserole. Let rest 10 minutes to set. Use a paper towel to dab off any additional moisture after resting time. Serve warm.

Bacon Cauli-Potato Mash

Mashed cauliflower can be a little thin on its own, but the single potato in this mouthwatering side dish adds just the amount of heft needed. This recipe still cuts back drastically on the glycemic index and the cauliflower is loaded with nutrition. And then the bacon... Enough said about that.

- **Hands-On Time: 15 minutes**
- **Cook Time: 9 minutes**

Serves 4

4 slices bacon, diced

2 cups chicken broth

1 small head cauliflower, chopped

1 russet potato, peeled and diced

3 cloves garlic, minced

1 teaspoon sea salt

½ teaspoon freshly ground black pepper

2 tablespoons ghee

¼ cup unsweetened almond milk

4 teaspoons chopped fresh chives

1 Press the Sauté button on the Instant Pot®. Add bacon and cook 3–4 minutes to render fat. Transfer bacon to a plate lined with paper towels.

2 Add broth to pot and scrape up any bits from the bottom and sides of the pot. Add cauliflower, potato, garlic, salt, and pepper. Lock lid. Press the Manual or Pressure Cook button and adjust time to 5 minutes. When timer beeps, quick-release pressure until float valve drops and then unlock lid.

3 Use an immersion blender to blend the mixture in the pot. Add ghee. Blend a little more. Add almond milk 1 tablespoon at a time, blending after each addition. You may need a little more or less almond milk depending on your desired consistency. Garnish with chives and serve warm.

Red Onion and Apple Confit

The sweetness from the caramelized onions and apple are the perfect match to be served with a salty and hearty pork chop. This is also nice alongside scrambled eggs and leftover beef in the morning.

- **Hands-On Time: 10 minutes**
- **Cook Time: 14 minutes**

Serves 4

2 tablespoons ghee

1 large red onion, peeled, halved, and sliced into half-moons

2 large Granny Smith apples, peeled, cored, and thinly sliced

2 tablespoons apple cider vinegar

2 tablespoons honey

½ teaspoon sea salt

¼ teaspoon freshly ground black pepper

¼ cup water

1 Press the Sauté button on the Instant Pot® and heat ghee. Add onion and apples; stir-fry 4–5 minutes until onions are translucent.

2 Add remaining ingredients to pot. Lock lid. Press the Manual or Pressure Cook button and adjust time to 10 minutes. When timer beeps, quick-release pressure until float valve drops and then unlock lid.

3 Simmer unlidded if there is any liquid remaining until it cooks off. Transfer mixture to a lidded container and refrigerate up to 1 week.

Sesame Zoodles

These zucchini zoodles are an excellent substitute and complement to the zippy sesame sauce, and it's prepared in no time flat. This dish pairs nicely with a steak or chicken dish... and don't forget your chopsticks!

- **Hands-On Time: 10 minutes**
- **Cook Time: 10 minutes**

Serves 4

¼ cup water

4 cups spiraled zucchini (about 3 small zucchini)

¼ cup coconut aminos

2 tablespoons pure maple syrup

1 teaspoon sriracha

2 teaspoons sesame oil

1 tablespoon creamy almond butter

¼ cup diced green onions

1 tablespoon toasted sesame seeds

1 Add water to the Instant Pot® and insert steamer basket.

2 In a large bowl, combine zucchini, coconut aminos, syrup, sriracha, sesame oil, almond butter, and green onions. Place the marinated zucchini in the steamer basket. Pour remaining marinade over zucchini. Lock lid. Press the Steam button and adjust time to 10 minutes. When timer beeps, quick-release pressure until float valve drops and then unlock lid.

3 Transfer zucchini to a serving bowl. Garnish with toasted sesame seeds. Serve immediately.

DON'T HAVE A SPIRALIZER?

If you don't own a spiralizer, you have a couple of options. First, most supermarkets carry a variety of spiraled vegetables, both in the produce and freezer sections. Second, you can use a vegetable peeler/knife to create your own "noodles."

Saffron and Herb Cauliflower Rice

This recipe is so, so easy and pairs nicely with seafood. Top this cauliflower rice with shrimp, mussels, sausage, and some asparagus for a quick paleo paella. Don't forget the fruit-packed sangria to accompany this dish.

- **Hands-On Time: 10 minutes**
- **Cook Time: 2 minutes**

Serves 4

1 cup water
1 medium head cauliflower, cut into florets
1 tablespoon ghee
2 cloves garlic, minced
½ teaspoon saffron threads
2 tablespoons chopped fresh Italian flat-leaf parsley
2 tablespoons chopped fresh basil
1 teaspoon sea salt
Pinch freshly ground black pepper
1 teaspoon lemon juice
½ teaspoon lemon zest

1 Add water to the Instant Pot® and insert steamer basket. Add cauliflower. Lock lid. Press the Steam button and adjust time for 2 minutes. When timer beeps, quick-release pressure until float valve drops and then unlock lid.

2 Transfer cauliflower to a serving bowl and discard liquid from pot.

3 Press the Sauté button on the Instant Pot® and heat ghee. Add cauliflower. Use a potato masher to smash cauliflower in the pot until it has a rice-like consistency.

4 Add remaining ingredients and stir. Transfer "rice" to a dish and serve warm.

Broccoli-Parsnip Smash

Listen up broccoli haters: This side dish is sure to become a new favorite. The parsnips and almond milk together lend a creamy texture and added flavor to an otherwise boring vegetable. Also, heads of broccoli come in so many sizes, so season with salt and pepper to taste. This recipe is merely a guideline.

- **Hands-On Time: 10 minutes**
- **Cook Time: 2 minutes**

Serves 4

1 cup water
1 medium head broccoli, cut into florets
2 parsnips, peeled and diced
2 teaspoons ghee
2 teaspoons nutritional yeast
2 tablespoons unsweetened almond milk
½ teaspoon sea salt
½ teaspoon freshly ground black pepper

1 Add water to the Instant Pot® and insert steamer basket. Add broccoli and parsnips. Lock lid. Press the Steam button and adjust time for 2 minutes. When timer beeps, quick-release pressure until float valve drops and then unlock lid.

2 Transfer broccoli and parsnips to a medium bowl and drain pot.

3 Press the Sauté button on the Instant Pot® and heat ghee. Add broccoli and parsnips. Use a potato masher to smash the vegetables in the pot until somewhat smooth.

4 Add yeast and milk. Smash it into broccoli mixture. Transfer to a serving bowl and season with salt and pepper. Serve warm.

6

Poultry Main Dishes

This chapter covers Cornish hens, turkey, and probably one of the most consumed proteins in the United States, chicken. There are so many recipes out there and a handful of go-to meals that you can cook for your family, but if you're sick of eating dried-out chicken breasts and overcooked thighs, the Instant Pot® is your new best friend. The steam and pressure used to cook ingredients in the pot are guaranteed to leave the chicken dishes in this chapter juicy and delicious. Whether you're craving Jamaican Jerk Chicken Meatballs or Kimchi Chicken Wings, or your family is calling for Chili-Orange Turkey Wings or Cornish Hens and Veggies, you'll find a new favorite recipe here!

Also, if you're planning on getting home late, the Instant Pot® allows you to start a meal in the morning and set it to automatically switch to the Keep Warm function for up to 10 hours, which means dinner will be ready and waiting when you walk in the door. So get cooking!

BBQ Whole Chicken

Sure, you can take extra time and stop at the grocery store on your way home from work, circle the parking lot a few times, and grab a rotisserie chicken. Or you can set the timer on your Instant Pot® and have a beautiful barbecue-rubbed whole chicken waiting for you and your family. And don't forget to save those bones to make some health-filled broth.

- **Hands-On Time: 10 minutes**
- **Cook Time: 25 minutes**

Serves 4

1 tablespoon smoked paprika

1 teaspoon espresso powder

1 teaspoon garlic powder

1 teaspoon sea salt

1 teaspoon freshly ground black pepper

½ teaspoon cayenne pepper

1 tablespoon pure maple syrup

1 (5-pound) whole chicken

1 small red apple, peeled, quartered, and cored

1 small orange, quartered

1 medium sweet onion, peeled and roughly chopped

3 cloves garlic, halved

2 cups water

1. In a small bowl, combine paprika, espresso powder, garlic powder, salt, black pepper, and cayenne pepper.

2. Brush the syrup on the outside of the chicken. Sprinkle prepared dry rub evenly over chicken. Place the apple and orange in the cavity of the bird.

3. Place onion and garlic in the bottom of the Instant Pot®. Pour in water. Insert trivet over vegetables.

4. Place chicken on trivet. Lock lid. Press the Manual or Pressure Cook button and adjust time to 25 minutes. When timer beeps, let pressure release naturally until float valve drops and then unlock lid. Check the chicken using a meat thermometer to ensure the internal temperature is at least 165°F.

5. Remove chicken. Discard apple and orange. Serve warm.

Gluten-Free Beer Can Dijon Chicken

A "beer can chicken" dish typically entails a beer can placed in the cavity of a chicken and then grilled or baked. The purpose is to utilize the steamed flavor from the beer. In this Instant Pot® twist, the flavor is distributed while the beer steams around the chicken. Change up the beer variety for a different flavor experience each time.

- **Hands-On Time: 10 minutes**
- **Cook Time: 20 minutes**

Serves 4

¼ cup Dijon mustard

3 pounds (about 10) chicken legs/drumsticks

1 large yellow onion, peeled and chopped

1 (12-ounce) bottle gluten-free beer, type of choice

1 Rub mustard over chicken legs.

2 Scatter onion in the bottom of the Instant Pot® and insert trivet. Add beer. Press the Sauté button and simmer unlidded 5 minutes.

3 Press the Adjust button and change temperature to Less. Arrange chicken standing up, meaty side down, on the trivet. Lock lid. Press the Poultry button and cook for the default time of 15 minutes. When timer beeps, quick-release pressure until float valve drops and then unlock lid. Check the chicken using a meat thermometer to ensure the internal temperature is at least 165°F.

4 Transfer chicken to a serving platter. Serve warm.

Kimchi Chicken Wings

Fermented foods are high on the "yes" list of the paleo diet. Kimchi, along with kombucha, sauerkraut, and pickles to name a few, have many health benefits. The probiotics in fermented foods aid in digestion and immunity and assist in the absorption of the nutrients in other foods you eat.

- **Hands-On Time: 10 minutes**
- **Cook Time: 8 minutes**

Serves 3

1½ pounds chicken wings, separated at the joint if necessary
½ cup kimchi brine
1 cup water
1 cup kimchi

WHAT IS KIMCHI?

Kimchi is a fermented spicy cabbage popular as a Korean side dish. Whether you are making your own or picking up a premade jar, there are a zillion variations available. There are varieties with cucumbers, radishes, and even different types of cabbage. The spices and chilies can vary as well. If you don't like one, try another. You just might be surprised.

1 Add chicken wings and kimchi brine to a large plastic bag. Seal and shake. Refrigerate at least 30 minutes up to 2 hours.

2 Add water to the Instant Pot® and insert steamer basket. Add chicken wings to basket and pour in extra brine from the plastic bag. Lock lid. Press the Manual or Pressure Cook button and adjust time to 8 minutes. When timer beeps, quick-release pressure until float valve drops and then unlock lid.

3 Transfer chicken wings to a large bowl and serve with kimchi.

Chicken Leg Almond Butter Satay

Satay is traditionally a peanut-based sauce, but because of the phytic acids in nuts, it isn't a paleo-friendly item. In this satay, almond butter is substituted in the marinade to mimic the same texture and flavor of the nuts.

- **Hands-On Time: 10 minutes**
- **Cook Time: 26 minutes**

Serves 5

½ cup smooth almond butter
¼ cup canned coconut milk
¼ cup coconut aminos
⅛ cup lime juice
1 teaspoon minced ginger
½ teaspoon fish sauce
1 teaspoon honey
½ teaspoon sea salt
3 pounds (about 10) chicken legs/drumsticks
1 cup water

1 In a medium bowl, whisk together almond butter, coconut milk, coconut aminos, lime juice, ginger, fish sauce, honey, and salt. Pour into a shallow dish with drumsticks. Cover and refrigerate overnight.

2 Add water to the Instant Pot® and insert trivet. Arrange chicken standing up, meaty side down, on the trivet. Lock lid. Press the Poultry button and cook for the default time of 15 minutes. When timer beeps, let pressure release naturally for 5 minutes. Quick-release any remaining pressure until float valve drops and then unlock lid. Check the chicken using a meat thermometer to ensure the internal temperature is at least 165°F.

3 While the Instant Pot® is releasing pressure, preheat oven to 550°F.

4 Place chicken legs on a baking sheet and broil 3 minutes on each side to crisp the chicken.

5 Transfer chicken to a serving plate and serve warm.

Smoked Paprika and Garlic Chicken Legs

Smoked paprika is an underused spice that should be at the front of your spice drawer. Sweet and smoky and a little mild, smoked paprika adds comfort to proteins and sauces, and it is lovely as a garnish on deviled eggs.

- **Hands-On Time: 5 minutes**
- **Cook Time: 21 minutes**

Serves 5

1 tablespoon garlic powder
1 tablespoon smoked paprika
1 teaspoon fine sea salt
3 pounds (about 10) chicken legs/drumsticks
1 cup water

1 Preheat oven to 550°F.

2 In a small bowl, combine garlic powder, smoked paprika, and salt. Season chicken legs with the seasoning mix.

3 Add water to the Instant Pot® and insert trivet. Arrange chicken standing up, meaty side down, on the trivet. Lock lid. Press the Poultry button and cook for the default time of 15 minutes. When timer beeps, let pressure release naturally for 5 minutes. Quick-release any remaining pressure until float valve drops and then unlock lid. Check the chicken using a meat thermometer to ensure the internal temperature is at least 165°F.

4 Place chicken legs on a baking sheet and broil 3 minutes on each side to crisp the chicken.

5 Transfer chicken to a serving plate and serve warm.

Chili Lime Chicken Legs

Sweet and tangy, salty and spicy, these Chili Lime Chicken Legs do a little dance on your taste buds. What an ideal recipe for outdoor socializing on the deck with close friends and a cooler full of ice-cold gluten-free beer.

- **Hands-On Time: 10 minutes**
- **Cook Time: 26 minutes**

Serves 5

2 tablespoons fresh lime juice

1 teaspoon lime zest

1 teaspoon chili powder

1 teaspoon sriracha

2 teaspoons honey

4 cloves garlic, minced

1 teaspoon sea salt

3 pounds (about 10) chicken legs/drumsticks

1 cup water

1 Preheat oven to 550°F.

2 In a medium bowl, combine lime juice, lime zest, chili powder, sriracha, honey, garlic, and salt. Toss chicken legs in the marinade. Refrigerate covered at least 1 hour or up to overnight.

3 Add water to the Instant Pot® and insert trivet. Arrange chicken standing up, meaty side down, on the trivet. Lock lid. Press the Poultry button and cook for the default time of 15 minutes. When timer beeps, let pressure release naturally for 5 minutes. Quick-release any remaining pressure until float valve drops and then unlock lid. Check the chicken using a meat thermometer to ensure the internal temperature is at least 165°F.

4 Place chicken legs on a baking sheet and broil 3 minutes on each side to crisp the chicken.

5 Transfer chicken to a serving plate and serve warm.

Kombucha Chicken Thighs

Kombucha, a popular fermented drink among paleo enthusiasts, comes in many flavors. When it all boils down, kombucha is an acid. So, if you have some chicken thighs and are left without a marinade, grab one of your kombucha drinks from the refrigerator. It will add a deeper flavor than just salt and pepper. The recipe calls for Gingerberry, but use what you have on hand for a different experience each time.

- **Hands-On Time: 5 minutes**
- **Cook Time: 7 minutes**

Serves 3

1½ pounds boneless, skinless chicken thighs

2 cups Gingerberry kombucha

1 teaspoon sea salt

1 Place chicken thighs and kombucha in a medium bowl. Refrigerate 1 hour.

2 Insert steamer basket in the Instant Pot®. Place chicken thighs evenly on basket. Pour in remaining kombucha marinade. Season chicken with salt. Lock lid. Press the Manual or Pressure Cook button and adjust time to 7 minutes. When timer beeps, quick-release pressure until float valve drops and then unlock lid. Check the chicken using a meat thermometer to ensure the internal temperature is at least 165°F.

3 Transfer chicken to a tray and serve warm.

Chicken Thighs with Strawberry Salsa

The sweetness of the strawberries plays nicely in this salsa with the bite of the red onion, the zest of the lime, and the creaminess of the avocado. If you prepare this ahead of time, make sure to toss in the avocado right before serving to avoid browning.

- **Hands-On Time: 10 minutes**
- **Cook Time: 7 minutes**

Serves 8

Strawberry Salsa
1 cup diced strawberries
½ cup fresh lime juice
1 tablespoon lime zest
2 Roma tomatoes, seeded and diced
¼ cup finely diced red onion
1 medium avocado, peeled, pitted, and diced
¼ cup chopped fresh cilantro
¼ cup chopped fresh mint
1 teaspoon sea salt

Chicken
3 pounds boneless, skinless chicken thighs
1 teaspoon sea salt
½ teaspoon freshly ground black pepper
1 cup water

1. In a large bowl, combine strawberries, lime juice, lime zest, tomatoes, onion, avocado, cilantro, mint, and salt. Refrigerate salsa covered at least 1 hour or up to overnight.

2. Pat chicken thighs dry with a paper towel. Season with salt and pepper.

3. Add water to the Instant Pot® and insert trivet. Place steamer basket on the trivet. Arrange thighs evenly on steamer basket. Lock lid. Press the Manual or Pressure Cook button and adjust time to 7 minutes. When timer beeps, quick-release pressure until float valve drops and then unlock lid. Check the chicken using a meat thermometer to ensure the internal temperature is at least 165°F.

4. Transfer chicken to plates. Garnish with strawberry salsa. Serve.

FRUIT SALSAS

Don't limit yourself to strawberries. Pineapple salsa pairs nicely with a grilled pork chop. And don't forget to grill your fruit before chopping it up for salsa. The heat caramelizes the natural sugars for an added level of flavor. Peaches and mangoes are two other tasty alternatives.

Tuscan Chicken

A taste of Italy can be on your dinner table in less than a half hour. And the thrilling part is that there will only be one cooking pot to wash at the end of the evening. The prosciutto and capers add a unique salty, earthy flavor that tops off this healthy meal.

- **Hands-On Time: 10 minutes**
- **Cook Time: 24 minutes**

Serves 4

1 tablespoon avocado oil

1 medium yellow onion, peeled and roughly diced

½ cup sliced cremini mushrooms

1 (14.5-ounce) can diced tomatoes, including juice

¼ cup chopped fresh basil

Pinch sea salt

1 pound boneless, skinless chicken breasts, cut into 1" cubes

4 ounces prosciutto, torn into pieces

1 tablespoon capers, drained

1 Press the Sauté button on the Instant Pot® and heat oil. Add onion and mushrooms and stir-fry 3–4 minutes until onions are translucent.

2 Add tomatoes, basil, salt, and chicken to pot. Lock lid. Press the Poultry button and cook for the default time of 15 minutes. When timer beeps, let pressure release naturally for 5 minutes. Quick-release any remaining pressure until float valve drops and then unlock lid. Check the chicken using a meat thermometer to ensure the internal temperature is at least 165°F.

3 Evenly distribute chicken mixture and sauce among four serving bowls. Garnish with prosciutto and capers.

Salsa Verde Chicken Meatballs

Zero carbs and gluten-free, who knew chicken meatballs could be so mouthwatering? The diced onion helps keep the ground chicken moist and the Salsa Verde is the perfect flavorful mild sauce to accompany this dish. Plus, what a great way to get the children involved in the kitchen. What child doesn't want to help make a creepalicious green sauce?

- **Hands-On Time: 15 minutes**
- **Cook Time: 16 minutes**

Yields 16 meatballs

1 pound ground chicken
1 large egg
½ cup chopped fresh mint
¼ cup almond meal
2 tablespoons finely diced Vidalia onion
1 teaspoon sea salt
¼ teaspoon freshly ground black pepper
2 tablespoons avocado oil, divided
½ cup water
1½ cups Salsa Verde (see Chapter 4)

1 In a medium bowl, combine ground chicken, egg, mint, almond meal, onion, salt, and pepper. Form into 16 golf ball–sized meatballs. Set aside.

2 Press the Sauté button on the Instant Pot® and heat 1 tablespoon oil. Place half the meatballs around the edges of the pot. Sear all sides of meatballs for a total of 4 minutes. Remove the first batch and set aside. Add remaining oil and meatballs and sear 4 minutes. Remove meatballs.

3 Discard extra juice and oil from the pot.

4 Add water to the Instant Pot® and insert steamer basket. Place meatballs evenly on steamer basket. Lock lid. Press the Manual or Pressure Cook button and adjust time to 3 minutes. When timer beeps, quick-release pressure until float valve drops and then unlock lid.

5 Drain the pot and add the meatballs. Pour in Salsa Verde. Let simmer 5 minutes, gently tossing meatballs.

6 Transfer meatballs and sauce to bowls and serve warm with sauce.

Honey Mustard Chicken Bites

Skip the fast-food fried nuggets. These chicken bites will be your kids' new favorite meal void of the preservatives, hydrogenated oils, and excessive sodium found in their quick-meal counterparts.

- **Hands-On Time: 10 minutes**
- **Cook Time: 25 minutes**

Serves 4

¼ cup honey

¼ cup yellow mustard

2 tablespoons mayonnaise

2 teaspoons apple cider vinegar

Pinch sea salt

1 pound boneless, skinless chicken breast, cut into 1" cubes

2 cups water

GROWN-UP CHICKEN BITES

If you want to kick up these kid-friendly Honey Mustard Chicken Bites a notch, try adding a squirt of sriracha to the sauce. Or replace the yellow mustard with some beer or horseradish mustard. Even more, substitute the honey with some maple syrup or molasses to add a different flavor profile.

1 In a medium bowl, whisk together honey, mustard, mayonnaise, vinegar, and salt. Set aside and refrigerate ¼ cup of the sauce for dipping. Toss chicken in remaining mixture and coat evenly. Cover and refrigerate 1 hour.

2 Add water to the Instant Pot® and insert steamer basket. Transfer chicken to steamer basket. Lock lid. Press the Poultry button and cook for the default time of 15 minutes. When timer beeps, let pressure release naturally for 10 minutes. Quick-release any remaining pressure until float valve drops and then unlock lid. Check the chicken using a meat thermometer to ensure the internal temperature is at least 165°F.

3 Serve warm with dipping sauce.

Jamaican Jerk Chicken Meatballs

Most Jamaican jerk seasoning blends already contain some dried chilies, so the habanero called for in this recipe is completely optional. If you aren't a fan of hot and spicy, eliminate the pepper. Otherwise, move on, mon, and enjoy these little jewels.

- **Hands-On Time: 15 minutes**
- **Cook Time: 11 minutes**

Yields 16 meatballs

1 pound ground chicken

1 large egg

1 tablespoon honey

¼ cup almond meal

1 tablespoon finely diced
   yellow onion

1 teaspoon finely diced
   habanero (seeded)

1 tablespoon Jamaican jerk
   seasoning blend

½ teaspoon sea salt

2 tablespoons avocado oil,
   divided

½ cup water

1 In a medium bowl, combine ground chicken, egg, honey, almond meal, onion, habanero, Jamaican jerk seasoning, and salt. Form into 16 golf ball–sized meatballs. Set aside.

2 Press the Sauté button on the Instant Pot® and heat 1 tablespoon oil. Place half the meatballs around the edges of the pot. Sear on all sides for a total of about 4 minutes. Remove the first batch and set aside. Add remaining oil and meatballs and sear 4 minutes. Remove meatballs.

3 Add water to the Instant Pot® and insert steamer basket. Place meatballs evenly on steamer basket. Lock lid.

4 Press the Manual or Pressure Cook button and adjust time to 3 minutes. When timer beeps, quick-release pressure until float valve drops and then unlock lid.

5 Transfer meatballs to a bowl and serve.

Taco Chicken Lettuce Wraps with Pico Guacamole

Gather the family around the table for Taco Tuesday. These lettuce wraps will hit the spot and there is no lack of flavor or nutrients. The ingredient list looks long, but most of the spices are already on your spice rack.

- **Hands-On Time: 10 minutes**
- **Cook Time: 15 minutes**

Serves 4

Pico Guacamole
Juice of 1 small lime

1 medium avocado, peeled and diced

2 cloves garlic, minced

1 small jalapeño, seeded and diced

¼ cup diced onion

2 tablespoons chopped fresh cilantro

2 Roma tomatoes, seeded and diced

Chicken
2 teaspoons chili powder

1 teaspoon ground cumin

1 teaspoon sea salt

½ teaspoon garlic powder

½ teaspoon smoked paprika

½ teaspoon ground coriander

1 pound boneless, skinless chicken breasts, cut into 1" cubes

2 cups water

8 iceberg lettuce leaves

1 Place lime and diced avocado in a medium bowl. Use a fork to smash the avocado until desired chunkiness. Add garlic, jalapeño, onion, salt, cilantro, and tomatoes. Refrigerate covered until ready to serve.

2 In a medium bowl, combine chili powder, cumin, salt, garlic powder, paprika, and coriander. Toss chicken into mixture and coat evenly.

3 Add water to the Instant Pot® and insert steamer basket. Transfer chicken to steamer basket. Lock lid. Press the Poultry button and cook for the default time of 15 minutes. When timer beeps, quick-release pressure until float valve drops and then unlock lid. Check the chicken using a meat thermometer to ensure the internal temperature is at least 165°F.

4 Transfer chicken to a cutting board and chop. Place in a serving bowl.

5 Serve chicken, lettuce leaves, and pico guacamole family-style.

Asian Chicken Lettuce Wraps with Ginger Aioli

These chicken lettuce wraps are packed with Asian flavors. If you ever have a friend tell you that paleo and gluten-free are boring and that they couldn't be on such a diet, serve them these lettuce wraps and watch the lightbulb turn on. There is no shortness of taste here.

- **Hands-On Time: 15 minutes**
- **Cook Time: 7 minutes**

Serves 4

Ginger Aioli
¼ cup mayonnaise
½ teaspoon minced ginger
⅛ teaspoon hot sauce
½ teaspoon lime juice

Lettuce Wraps
1 tablespoon sesame oil
1 pound ground chicken
⅓ cup chopped green onions
3 cloves garlic, minced
5 ounces shiitake mushrooms
1 tablespoon minced fresh
  ginger
¼ cup coconut aminos
1 teaspoon Dijon mustard
1 tablespoon sriracha
1 tablespoon honey
½ teaspoon sea salt
¼ teaspoon white pepper
1 cup water
12 Bibb lettuce leaves
¼ cup slivered almonds

1 In a small bowl, whisk together Ginger Aioli ingredients. Refrigerate covered until ready to use.

2 Press the Sauté button on the Instant Pot® and heat sesame oil. Add chicken and onions; stir-fry 4–5 minutes until onions are translucent. Transfer mixture to a 7-cup glass bowl. Stir in garlic, mushrooms, ginger, coconut aminos, mustard, sriracha, honey, salt, and pepper.

3 Add water to the Instant Pot® and insert trivet. Set bowl with chicken mixture on trivet. Lock lid. Press the Manual or Pressure Cook button and adjust time to 2 minutes. When timer beeps, quick-release pressure until float valve drops and then unlock lid.

4 Serve chicken mixture warm with lettuce leaves, slivered almonds, and Ginger Aioli on the side.

Chicken Livers and Onions with Gravy

Chicken liver usually brings up memories of our grandparents as that seems to be the generation that really embraced this particular offal. So, start your own memories, update this relic, and bring this nutritional dish back to the dinner table.

- **Hands-On Time: 10 minutes**
- **Cook Time: 12 minutes**

Serves 4

2 tablespoons ghee

2 medium yellow onions, peeled, halved, and thinly sliced

2 sprigs fresh rosemary

1 pound chicken livers, halved and trimmed

10 grape tomatoes, halved

½ cup beef broth

2 tablespoons cooking sherry

2 tablespoons cassava flour

½ teaspoon sea salt

2 tablespoons chopped fresh basil

1 Press the Sauté button on the Instant Pot® and heat ghee. Add onions and rosemary. Stir-fry 3 minutes. Add chicken livers and tomatoes and stir-fry an additional 3 minutes.

2 Add beef broth and cooking sherry to the pot. Lock lid. Press the Meat/Stew button and adjust time to 6 minutes. When timer beeps, quick-release pressure until float valve drops and then unlock lid.

3 Transfer chicken livers, onions, and tomatoes to a medium bowl.

4 Whisk flour and salt into pot juices until it thickens. Transfer to a gravy boat.

5 Garnish chicken livers with fresh basil and serve warm with gravy.

Avocado Chicken Salad

A fresh and quick meal, this chicken salad is also a great recipe to make on prep day to portion out for the remainder of the week. Whether for a light luncheon or weekday meal, this savory chicken dish is the ideal go-to recipe.

- **Hands-On Time: 10 minutes**
- **Cook Time: 5 minutes**

Serves 6

2 pounds chicken breasts, cut into 1" cubes
1 teaspoon fine sea salt
1 teaspoon freshly ground black pepper
1 cup water
½ medium red onion, peeled and diced
2 stalks celery, finely chopped
2 Roma tomatoes, seeded and diced
1 medium avocado, peeled and diced
½ cup mayonnaise
1 tablespoon yellow mustard
½ dried dill
½ teaspoon lime juice

1 On a plate, season chicken pieces with salt and pepper. Set aside.

2 Add water to the Instant Pot® and insert steamer basket. Place chicken cubes on steamer basket. Lock lid. Press the Manual or Pressure Cook button and adjust time to 5 minutes. When timer beeps, quick-release pressure until float valve drops and then unlock lid.

3 Transfer chicken to a cutting board. When cool enough to work with, finely chop the chicken. Add to a medium bowl.

4 Add onion, celery, tomatoes, avocado, mayonnaise, yellow mustard, dill, and lime juice. Refrigerate covered until ready to serve.

Paleo-ish Turkish Chicken Thighs

Like cheese and alcohol, yogurt is not allowed in the strict paleo world. However, if you are okay with including a minimal amount of dairy in your diet and you don't have gut issues or allergies, this recipe is a great option to add a little dairy into your life. The remaining plain yogurt can be turned into a tzatziki sauce for some lamb meatballs, or it can be added to fresh berries along with a drizzle of honey for a delicious breakfast, or it can just be added to a post-workout smoothie for a little added creaminess and protein!

- **Hands-On Time: 15 minutes**
- **Cook Time: 15 minutes**

Serves 8

1 cup plain Greek yogurt
¼ teaspoon ground coriander
¼ teaspoon ground nutmeg
¼ teaspoon ground cumin
¼ teaspoon ground cinnamon
½ teaspoon sea salt
3 pounds boneless, skinless chicken thighs
2 tablespoons avocado oil
3 large carrots, peeled and spiralized
2 cups water
¼ cup fresh chopped Italian flat-leaf parsley
¼ cup fresh chopped mint

1 In a large bowl, combine yogurt, coriander, nutmeg, cumin, cinnamon, and salt. Toss chicken thighs in sauce and refrigerate covered at least 4 hours or up to overnight.

2 Press the Sauté button on the Instant Pot®. Heat avocado oil and fry chicken thighs 2 minutes on each side until browned.

3 Insert steamer basket in the Instant Pot®; place chicken evenly on basket. Pour any remaining marinade over chicken. Lock lid. Press the Manual or Pressure Cook button and adjust time to 7 minutes. When timer beeps, quick-release pressure until float valve drops and then unlock lid. Check the chicken using a meat thermometer to make sure the internal temperature is at least 165°F.

4 Transfer chicken to a medium bowl. Set aside.

5 Add spiralized carrots to steamer basket. Add water and lock lid. Press the Sauté button and let carrots cook 3–5 minutes until tender.

6 Transfer carrots to individual bowls. Top with chicken. Garnish bowls with parsley and mint. Serve warm.

Cornish Hens and Veggies

Why is it that a whole chicken is an economical choice, but when miniaturized, Cornish hens are just a sexy meal for two or a fancy dish for guests? Either split the cooked hens in half and serve four guests with some extra sides or just enjoy them with the tender mushrooms and carrots with your sweetie.

- **Hands-On Time: 15 minutes**
- **Cook Time: 20 minutes**

Serves 2

2 Cornish hens (1½ pounds each)

1 pound whole button mushrooms, stems trimmed

3 large carrots, peeled and sliced into ½" sections

1½ cups water

1 teaspoon sea salt

1 teaspoon freshly ground black pepper

1 teaspoon smoked paprika

2 cloves garlic, halved

1 small Granny Smith apple, cored and quartered

1 Pat down Cornish hens with a paper towel. Set aside.

2 Place mushrooms, carrots, and water in the bottom of the Instant Pot®. Insert steamer basket.

3 In a small container, combine salt, pepper, and paprika. Season Cornish hens evenly with spice mix. Insert garlic and apple into the cavities of the hens.

4 Place hens on steamer basket. Press the Meat button and adjust time to 10 minutes. When timer beeps, let pressure release naturally for 5 minutes. Quick-release any remaining pressure until float valve drops and then unlock lid. Check the hens using a meat thermometer to make sure the internal temperature is at least 165°F.

5 Set oven to Broil.

6 Transfer hens to a baking sheet. Remove and discard apples and garlic. Broil 5 minutes.

7 Transfer hens to a serving platter. Use a slotted spoon to remove mushrooms and carrots from the pot and place them around the hens. Serve warm.

Chili-Orange Turkey Wings

Turkey isn't just for Thanksgiving. Check the meat section next time you are at the grocery store. Throughout the year, there will be turkey legs and breasts offered separately. Buying the whole bird isn't necessary. The sriracha-orange-honey seasoning trio provides a nice balance of spicy and tangy and sweet.

- **Hands-On Time: 10 minutes**
- **Cook Time: 15 minutes**

Serves 2

2 turkey wings (about 2½ pounds)
2 teaspoons sea salt
2 cups water
2 tablespoons freshly squeezed orange juice
1 teaspoon orange zest
2 tablespoons honey
1 tablespoon sriracha
2 teaspoons ghee

1 Pat down turkey wings with a paper towel. Season with salt.

2 Add water to the Instant Pot® and insert steamer basket. Place wings on steamer basket.

3 Press the Meat or Poultry button and adjust time to 10 minutes. When timer beeps, quick-release any remaining pressure until float valve drops and then unlock lid. Check the wings using a meat thermometer to make sure the internal temperature is at least 165°F.

4 Set oven to Broil.

5 In a large bowl, combine orange juice, orange zest, honey, sriracha, and ghee. Add turkey wings and toss to coat. Transfer wings to a baking sheet. Broil 5 minutes. Serve warm.

Mega Turkey Meatballs

You can call these mega meatballs or small meatloaves, but definitely try them. Served with your favorite sides, these meatballs are full of flavor from the fresh herbs. The onions and carrots work harmoniously to lend the moisture that the ground turkey needs to make this a delicious meal.

- **Hands-On Time: 15 minutes**
- **Cook Time: 15 minutes**

Yields 4 meatballs

1 pound ground turkey

1 large egg

1 teaspoon sea salt

¼ teaspoon freshly ground black pepper

¼ teaspoon garlic powder

½ cup almond meal

½ cup peeled and grated carrot

1 tablespoon finely diced yellow onion

2 tablespoons chopped fresh oregano

2 tablespoons chopped fresh Italian flat-leaf parsley

2 tablespoons avocado oil, divided

½ cup water

1 In a medium bowl, combine turkey, egg, salt, pepper, garlic powder, almond meal, carrot, onion, oregano, and parsley. Form into 4 large meatballs. Set aside.

2 Press the Sauté button on the Instant Pot® and heat 1 tablespoon oil. Place 2 meatballs in the pot. Sear all sides of the meatballs for a total of about 4 minutes. Remove the first batch and set aside. Add remaining oil and meatballs and sear an additional 4 minutes. Remove meatballs.

3 Add water to the Instant Pot® and insert steamer basket. Place meatballs evenly on steamer basket. Lock lid. Press the Manual or Pressure Cook button and adjust time to 6 minutes. When timer beeps, quick-release pressure until float valve drops and then unlock lid.

4 Transfer meatballs to plates. Serve warm.

7

Beef and Bison Main Dishes

There is nothing better suited for the Instant Pot® than meat. The steam and pressure can take a seemingly tough piece of meat and make it taste like butter in your mouth. The steam keeps everything moist, and the pressure helps break down some of the sinewy parts. And the best part? The trapped steam helps create a meat that tastes like it has been braised for hours in about 30 minutes, depending on the weight. In addition, you can add your potatoes, carrots, mushrooms, and other vegetables to the pot while cooking. Not only will you have a complete meal, but the vegetables take on a completely new savory flavor by cooking next to the meat, especially those mushrooms. With recipes ranging from Sweet-n-Spicy Beef Brisket and Skirt Steak Fajitas to Cuban Picadillo with Riced Cauliflower and Italian Beef Tongue Lettuce Wraps, this chapter will help get you started on some classic Instant Pot® recipes as well as introduce you to some new favorites.

Nana's Sunday Pot Roast

The salt and pepper simply bring out the natural goodness of the roast. The drippings give the vegetables a savory, rich, and earthy note. You'll feel like Nana is just around the corner!

- **Hands-On Time: 10 minutes**
- **Cook Time: 65 minutes**

Serves 6

1 (3-pound) pot roast

1 teaspoon sea salt

1 teaspoon freshly ground black pepper

2 tablespoons ghee

2 cups beef broth

2 large carrots, peeled and cut into 1" sections

3 russet potatoes, quartered

1 large yellow onion, peeled, halved, and sliced into half-moons

8 ounces whole button mushrooms, stems trimmed

1 tablespoon fresh thyme leaves

1   Pat roast dry with paper towels. Season with salt and pepper.

2   Press the Sauté button on the Instant Pot® and heat ghee. Sear meat on all sides, about 5 minutes. Remove the meat and set aside.

3   Add broth and deglaze the pot by stirring and scraping bottom and sides to loosen any browned bits. Add remaining ingredients. Return roast to pot. Press the Manual or Pressure Cook button and adjust time to 60 minutes. When timer beeps, let pressure release naturally until float valve drops and then unlock lid.

4   Remove the meat and vegetables to a serving platter. Let rest 5 minutes. Slice roast and serve warm.

Chuck Roast with Carrots and Onions

Oh, the humble chuck roast. It is usually overlooked because of toughness of the connective tissue that usually takes hours of low and slow cooking to dissolve. The Instant Pot® with its high pressure and steam takes care of this so much faster. Succulent and delicious, chuck roast is making a comeback!

- **Hands-On Time: 15 minutes**
- **Cook Time: 65 minutes**

Serves 6

1 (3-pound) boneless chuck roast
2 tablespoons horseradish mustard
1 teaspoon sea salt
½ teaspoon freshly ground black pepper
2 tablespoons avocado oil
2 cups beef broth
2 teaspoons Worcestershire sauce
1 medium yellow onion, peeled and diced
5 large carrots, peeled and cut into 1" sections

1 Pat roast dry with paper towels. Massage mustard into roast. Season with salt and pepper.

2 Press the Sauté button on the Instant Pot® and heat oil. Sear meat on all sides, about 5 minutes total. Remove the meat and set aside.

3 Add broth and deglaze the pot by scraping the bottom and sides of the pot to loosen any browned bits. Stir in Worcestershire sauce.

4 Add onion and carrots to pot. Place roast on top of vegetables. Press the Manual or Pressure Cook button and adjust time to 60 minutes. When timer beeps, let pressure release naturally until float valve drops and then unlock lid.

5 Transfer meat and vegetables to a serving platter. Let rest 5 minutes. Slice roast. Reserve some of the pot juices if you'd like to serve "au jus" with the meal. Serve warm.

Sweet-n-Spicy Beef Brisket

The Instant Pot® is a great way to dress up a cheaper cut of meat. Add some fabulous spices and this brisket is a five-star delight. Placing the brisket fat side down helps render some of that fat cap. Also, the maple syrup in the wet rub gets a good layer of caramelization for added flavor.

- **Hands-On Time: 10 minutes**
- **Cook Time: 66 minutes**

Serves 6

2 tablespoons pure maple syrup
2 tablespoons coconut aminos
1 tablespoon adobo paste
1 tablespoon yellow mustard
½ teaspoon garlic salt
1 tablespoon Italian seasoning
2 tablespoons coconut oil
1 (3-pound) beef brisket
1 cup water
1 large yellow onion, peeled and roughly diced

1 In a small bowl, whisk together syrup, coconut aminos, adobo paste, mustard, garlic salt, and Italian seasoning. Massage over beef brisket.

2 Press the Sauté button on the Instant Pot® and heat coconut oil. Adjust temperature to Less. Place brisket in the pot with the fat cap side down. Sear 6 minutes to render fat.

3 Add water and scatter onions around brisket. Press the Manual or Pressure Cook button and adjust time to 60 minutes. When timer beeps, let pressure release naturally until float valve drops and then unlock lid.

4 Remove the meat and transfer to a serving platter. Let rest 10 minutes. Slice brisket and serve warm.

Tender Flank Steak with Mushrooms and Onions

Peanut butter and jelly...Laverne and Shirley...tweens and boy bands. These are classic combinations. But, let's add another. Steak and mushrooms. The drippings from the steak add another dimension to these button mushrooms that is like no other. Simple. Quick. Delicious. It's hard to tell the star of this dish!

- **Hands-On Time: 10 minutes**
- **Cook Time: 50 minutes**

Serves 4

1 (2-pound) flank steak

1 teaspoon sea salt

½ teaspoon freshly ground black pepper

2 tablespoons avocado oil, divided

1 slice bacon, diced

1 medium yellow onion, peeled and diced

2 cups whole button mushrooms

1½ cups beef broth

1 Pat steak dry with paper towels. Season with salt and pepper.

2 Press the Sauté button on the Instant Pot® and heat 1 tablespoon oil. Sear meat on all sides until browned, about 5 minutes per side. Remove meat and set aside.

3 Add remaining oil to pot and sauté bacon, onions, and mushrooms 3–5 minutes until onions are translucent.

4 Add beef broth and deglaze the pot by stirring and scraping the bottom and sides of the pot to loosen any browned bits. Place meat on top of onions in pot. Lock lid. Press the Meat button and adjust time to 35 minutes. When timer beeps, let pressure release naturally until float valve drops and then unlock lid.

5 Transfer the meat to a serving platter. Let rest 5 minutes. Thinly slice meat against the grain. Serve immediately with mushrooms, onions, and a few tablespoons of the liquid from the pot.

Skirt Steak Fajitas

This simple dish with such depth of flavor can be enjoyed for dinner, lunch, or even for breakfast as most paleo folks like their leftover meat in the morning, served with a side of scrambled eggs and a thick slice of avocado. There are so many ways to enjoy this tasty beef so dive on in!

- **Hands-On Time: 15 minutes**
- **Cook Time: 45 minutes**

Serves 4

⅛ cup avocado oil

¼ cup coconut aminos

1 tablespoon fish sauce

1 teaspoon ground cumin

1 teaspoon chili powder

2 tablespoons tomato paste

½ teaspoon sea salt

1 (2-pound) skirt steak

1 small yellow onion, peeled and diced

1 medium green bell pepper, seeded and diced

1 medium red bell pepper, seeded and diced

1 cup beef broth

1   In a small bowl, combine oil, coconut aminos, fish sauce, cumin, chili powder, tomato paste, and salt. Spread ¾ of this mixture on all sides of the steak. Reserve additional sauce.

2   Press the Sauté button on the Instant Pot®. Add skirt steak and sear on all sides for a total of about 5 minutes. Remove the meat and set aside. Add onion and peppers to the pot with reserved sauce. Sauté 3–5 minutes until onions are translucent.

3   Add beef broth. Set meat on the layer of onion and peppers. Lock lid. Press the Meat button and cook for the default time of 35 minutes. When timer beeps, let pressure release naturally until float valve drops and then unlock lid.

4   Use a slotted spoon to transfer the meat and vegetables to a serving platter. Let steak rest 5 minutes. Thinly slice the skirt steak against the grain. Serve warm.

Korean Beef Short Ribs

Short ribs are just that: ribs taken from the short portion of the rib bone of cattle. There are two types of cuts with short ribs: flanken and English cut. For this recipe, flanken is the preferred choice. Your butcher can help achieve this if there are no prepackaged options. Otherwise, the sauce of this recipe will work to flavor any cut of meat you prefer.

- **Hands-On Time: 10 minutes**
- **Cook Time: 25 minutes**

Serves 4

¼ cup coconut aminos
¼ cup pure maple syrup
1 teaspoon fish sauce
1 tablespoon apple cider vinegar
1 tablespoon sesame oil
1 teaspoon white pepper
½ teaspoon ground ginger
½ teaspoon garlic powder
½ teaspoon sea salt
3 pounds beef short ribs
1 cup beef broth
2 green onions, sliced
1 tablespoon toasted sesame seeds

1 In a medium bowl, whisk together coconut aminos, syrup, fish sauce, vinegar, sesame oil, white pepper, ground ginger, garlic powder, and sea salt. Add ribs and toss to coat. Refrigerate covered at least 60 minutes or up to overnight.

2 Add beef broth to the Instant Pot® and insert trivet. Arrange ribs standing upright with the meaty side facing outward. Lock lid. Press the Manual or Pressure Cook button and adjust time to 25 minutes. When timer beeps, let pressure release naturally until float valve drops and then unlock lid.

3 Transfer ribs to a serving platter and garnish with green onions and sesame seeds. Serve warm.

Mongolian Beef and Cashew BBQ

Typically when you order this dish in restaurants, you go through the line and pick your meat, vegetables, oil, and sauces, and then hand it over to the chef who cooks it right in front of you. Cashews are actually in the paleo-ish category, because they are technically a legume. They fall more into the "primal" category. So, if you choose to indulge, purchase them raw so as to avoid the highly processed versions.

- **Hands-On Time: 15 minutes**
- **Cook Time: 10 minutes**

Serves 4

1 tablespoon sesame oil

1 (2-pound) skirt steak

¼ cup coconut aminos

½ cup pure maple syrup

1" piece fresh ginger, peeled and grated

4 cloves garlic, minced

½ cup plus 2 tablespoons water, divided

2 tablespoons arrowroot flour

¼ cup sliced green onions

¼ cup crushed raw cashews

1 Press the Sauté button on the Instant Pot®. Heat oil and sear steak on all sides, for a total of about 4 minutes. Transfer steak to a cutting board. Slice beef against the grain into thin strips. Return beef to pot.

2 In a medium bowl, whisk together coconut aminos, syrup, ginger, garlic, and ½ cup water. Pour over beef and stir to deglaze any bits around the edges and bottom of the Instant Pot®. Lock lid. Press the Manual or Pressure Cook button and adjust time to 0 minutes. When timer beeps, quick-release pressure until float valve drops and then unlock lid.

3 In a small dish, whisk together arrowroot flour and 2 tablespoons water until smooth to create a slurry. Stir this mixture into the beef mixture. Press the Sauté button, then adjust temperature to Less and simmer unlidded 5 minutes until the sauce thickens.

4 Ladle mixture into bowls. Garnish with green onions and raw cashews. Serve warm.

Meatloaf and Gravy

Meatloaf is a worldwide tradition. It seems that every country in the world has a variation on this simple dish. As long as you have some form of ground meat, vegetables, and a binding agent, a meatloaf can be made. This quick and easy meatloaf is the perfect weeknight staple, especially when served with potatoes and vegetables.

- **Hands-On Time: 10 minutes**
- **Cook Time: 35 minutes**

Serves 6

1 pound ground beef

1 pound ground pork

3 large eggs

1 large shallot, peeled and finely diced

½ cup tomato sauce

½ cup almond meal

1 tablespoon Italian seasoning

½ teaspoon smoked paprika

½ teaspoon garlic powder

1 teaspoon sea salt

½ teaspoon freshly ground black pepper

1 cup beef broth

1 tablespoon cassava flour

2 tablespoons unsweetened almond milk

1 In a large bowl, combine beef, pork, eggs, shallot, tomato sauce, almond meal, Italian seasoning, smoked paprika, garlic powder, salt, and pepper. Form mixture into a ball and flatten the top. Place meatloaf in a lightly greased 7-cup bowl.

2 Add beef broth to the Instant Pot® and insert trivet. Place the glass bowl on top. Lock lid. Press the Meat button and cook for the default time of 35 minutes. When timer beeps, quick-release any remaining pressure until float valve drops and then unlock lid.

3 Remove meatloaf from Instant Pot® and let cool at room temperature 10 minutes. Tilt glass bowl and pour any liquid/rendered fat back into the pot.

4 Whisk flour and milk into the pot juices until a thick gravy forms. Transfer to a gravy boat.

5 Slice meatloaf and serve with gravy.

UTENSIL HACKS

You may want to fashion an aluminum foil sling for easy retrieval if you don't have a pair of plate retriever tongs. Take a 10" × 10" square of aluminum foil and fold it back and forth until you have a 2" × 10" sling. Place sling under the bowl or pan before cooking so that you can easily lift up the heated dish when cooking is complete.

Balsamic Meatballs

So, there is a little debate over whether balsamic vinegar is officially a "paleo" product. I'm sure for the strictest of strict, the answer is probably no. Although vinegars have some wonderful health benefits, they are not all created equally. Some of the cheaper versions are laced with added sugars and caramel coloring. So, heed caution, read your labels, and go forth and conquer this recipe!

- **Hands-On Time: 15 minutes**
- **Cook Time: 11 minutes**

Yields 16 meatballs

1 pound ground beef

1 large egg

2 tablespoons finely diced shallot

1 tablespoon Italian seasoning

1 teaspoon garlic powder

½ teaspoon celery seed

½ teaspoon smoked paprika

¼ cup almond meal

2 tablespoons avocado oil, divided

2 cups water

1 cup Marinara Sauce (see Chapter 4)

2 tablespoons balsamic vinegar

2 tablespoons julienned fresh basil

1 In a medium bowl, combine beef, egg, shallot, Italian seasoning, garlic powder, celery seed, smoked paprika, and almond meal. Form into 16 meatballs. Set aside.

2 Press the Sauté button on the Instant Pot® and heat 1 tablespoon oil. Place half the meatballs around the edges of the pot and sear on all sides for a total of about 4 minutes. Remove the first batch and set aside. Add remaining oil and meatballs and sear 4 minutes. Remove meatballs from pot.

3 In a small bowl, combine marinara sauce and balsamic vinegar. Add seared meatballs to a 7-cup glass bowl. Gently toss in marinara-balsamic sauce to coat meatballs evenly.

4 Add water to the Instant Pot® and insert steamer basket. Place meatballs evenly on steamer basket. Press the Manual or Pressure Cook button and adjust time to 3 minutes. When timer beeps, quick-release pressure until float valve drops and then unlock lid.

5 Remove dish from the pot. Garnish with fresh basil and serve warm.

Marinara Meatballs

Now that's a good meatball! The homemade Marinara Sauce (see Chapter 4) really makes the meal. There is something about homemade foods and sauces that make you want to cook fresh every day. And, with the Instant Pot®, this is feasible with the time on cooked foods cut by at least half.

- **Hands-On Time: 15 minutes**
- **Cook Time: 16 minutes**

Yields 16 meatballs

1 pound ground chuck
1 large egg
½ cup chopped fresh basil
¼ cup almond meal
2 tablespoons finely diced yellow onion
½ teaspoon garlic powder
1 teaspoon sea salt
¼ teaspoon freshly ground black pepper
2 tablespoons avocado oil, divided
½ cup water
1½ cups Marinara Sauce (see Chapter 4)

1 In a medium bowl, combine ground chuck, egg, basil, almond meal, onion, garlic powder, salt, and pepper. Form into 16 golf ball–sized meatballs. Set aside.

2 Press the Sauté button on the Instant Pot® and heat 1 tablespoon oil. Place half the meatballs around the edges of the pot. Sear all sides of the meatballs for a total of about 4 minutes total. Remove the first batch and set aside. Add remaining oil and meatballs and sear 4 minutes. Remove meatballs.

3 Discard extra juice and oil from the pot. Add water to the Instant Pot® and insert steamer basket. Place meatballs evenly on steamer basket. Lock lid. Press the Manual or Pressure Cook button and adjust time to 3 minutes. When timer beeps, quick-release pressure until float valve drops and then unlock lid.

4 Drain the pot. Add meatballs directly to the pot. Pour in Marinara Sauce. Let simmer 5 minutes, gently tossing meatballs.

5 Transfer meatballs and sauce to bowls and serve warm.

Reuben Meatballs with Russian Dressing

Oh, the Reuben sandwich. Although these meatballs are void of the rye bread and ooey-gooey Swiss cheese, this meatball will hopefully quench that craving for the deli delight. Corned beef and sauerkraut are mixed directly in the ground beef. Caraway seeds are added to hit that "rye bread" flavor. And the Russian Dressing pulls it all together!

- Hands-On Time: 15 minutes
- Cook Time: 11 minutes

Yields 24 meatballs

Russian Dressing
½ cup mayonnaise

2 tablespoons paleo ketchup

1 small shallot, peeled and minced

1 tablespoon lemon juice

1 teaspoon prepared horseradish

½ teaspoon smoked paprika

¼ teaspoon sea salt

Meatballs
1 pound ground beef

½ pound finely chopped corned beef

½ cup finely chopped sauerkraut, drained (plus extra for garnish if desired)

¼ cup almond meal

2 tablespoons German mustard

1 tablespoon caraway seeds

1 large egg

½ teaspoon sea salt

¼ teaspoon freshly ground black pepper

2 tablespoons avocado oil

1 cup water

1 In a small bowl, combine Russian Dressing ingredients and refrigerate covered until ready to use.

2 In a medium bowl, combine ground beef, corned beef, sauerkraut, almond meal, mustard, caraway seeds, egg, salt, and pepper. Form into 24 golf ball–sized meatballs. Set aside.

3 Press the Sauté button on the Instant Pot® and heat 1 tablespoon of the oil. Place half the meatballs around the edges of the pot and sear on all sides, for a total of about 4 minutes. Remove the first batch and set aside. Add remaining oil and meatballs and sear 4 minutes. Remove meatballs.

4 Discard extra juice and oil from the Instant Pot®.

5 Add water to the Instant Pot® and insert steamer basket. Place meatballs evenly on steamer basket. Lock lid. Press the Manual or Pressure Cook button and adjust time to 3 minutes. When timer beeps, quick-release pressure until float valve drops and then unlock lid.

6 Transfer meatballs to a tray and serve with Russian Dressing on the side. Garnish with extra sauerkraut if desired.

Ground Beef and Broccoli Bowl

Typically Beef and Broccoli is made with steak; however, this version not only is economical by substituting ground chuck, but is quick and easy to prepare with minimal cleanup.

- **Hands-On Time: 10 minutes**
- **Cook Time: 4 minutes**

Serves 2

¼ cup coconut aminos
2 tablespoons fish sauce
¼ teaspoon white pepper
4 cloves garlic, minced
1 tablespoon cooking sherry
2 tablespoons beef broth
1 tablespoon avocado oil
1 pound ground chuck
1 bunch green onions, sliced (reserve 2 tablespoons chopped greens for garnish)
1 head broccoli, cut in bite-sized pieces

1 In a small bowl, combine coconut aminos, fish sauce, white pepper, garlic, sherry, and beef broth. Set aside.

2 Press the Sauté button on the Instant Pot® and heat oil. Add ground chuck and green onions; stir-fry 4 minutes until onions are tender and beef is almost all brown.

3 Add sauce mixture and toss to combine. Add broccoli. Lock lid. Press the Manual or Pressure Cook button and adjust time to 0 minutes. When timer beeps, quick-release pressure until float valve drops and then unlock lid.

4 Transfer pot ingredients to two serving bowls. Garnish with green onions. Serve warm.

Just Beet It Burgers

Jazz up your ho-hum burgers by adding some beets to your ground beef. The sweetness of the beets pairs nicely with the garlic and cayenne. And it's always nice to hide vegetables in meals for picky eaters, especially dishes packed with vitamin C and essential minerals.

- **Hands-On Time: 10 minutes**
- **Cook Time: 11 minutes**

Serves 4

1 pound ground chuck
½ cup scrubbed and grated beets
1 teaspoon cooking sherry
½ teaspoon garlic powder
½ teaspoon sea salt
½ teaspoon freshly ground black pepper
⅛ teaspoon cayenne pepper
2 tablespoons coconut oil, divided
1 cup water

1 In a medium bowl, combine ground chuck, beets, cooking sherry, garlic powder, salt, pepper, and cayenne pepper. Form into 4 burger patties. Set aside.

2 Press the Sauté button on the Instant Pot® and heat 1 tablespoon oil. Place 2 patties in the pot. Sear the burgers 2 minutes on each side. Remove the patties and set aside. Add remaining oil and remaining patties and sear 2 minutes on each side. Set aside.

3 Add water to the Instant Pot® and insert steamer basket. Prop patties evenly on steamer basket. Lock lid. Press the Manual or Pressure Cook button and adjust time to 3 minutes. When timer beeps, quick-release pressure until float valve drops and then unlock lid.

4 Transfer patties to serving plates. Serve warm.

Corned Beef and Cabbage

It just isn't St. Paddy's Day without a little corned beef and cabbage. While drinking your black and tan, let the Instant Pot® do the legwork, allowing you time to do an Irish jig with your friends. The corned beef brisket even comes with its own spice packet, so sit back, kiss the Blarney Stone, and wait for dinner to be cooked for you!

- **Hands-On Time: 15 minutes**
- **Cook Time: 75 minutes**

Serves 6

3-pound corned beef brisket with spice packet

2 tablespoons avocado oil

1 large yellow onion, peeled and quartered

4 large carrots, peeled and cut into 2" sections

1 small cabbage, cut into 6 wedges

3 cloves garlic, smashed and quartered

1 cup beef broth

1 cup water

1 Massage contents of spice packet over corned beef brisket.

2 Press the Sauté button on the Instant Pot® and heat avocado oil. Add brisket and sear on all sides 6–7 minutes. Transfer brisket to a plate.

3 Add onion to the pot and stir-fry 3–4 minutes until tender. Add remaining ingredients, including brisket, to Instant Pot®. Lock lid. Press the Meat/Stew button and cook for the default time of 45 minutes. When timer beeps, naturally release pressure for 20 minutes. Quick-release any remaining pressure until float valve drops and then unlock lid.

4 Transfer brisket to a cutting board. When cooled enough to work with, slice and transfer to a serving tray. Add vegetables and serve warm.

Cuban Picadillo with Riced Cauliflower

Traditionally served over rice, cauliflower is a perfect grain-free replacement. To "rice" the cauliflower, simply use a box grater until you achieve 3 cups. You will heat this in the pot liquid at the very end of cooking process until tender.

- **Hands-On Time: 15 minutes**
- **Cook Time: 8 minutes**

Serves 4

1 tablespoon coconut oil
1 pound ground beef
1 medium yellow onion, peeled and diced
1 medium parsnip, peeled and diced
2 cloves garlic, minced
½ cup dry white wine
2 tablespoons tomato paste
1 teaspoon ground cumin
½ teaspoon sea salt
1 teaspoon dried oregano
¼ cup sliced green olives
1 tablespoon capers
1 teaspoon caper juice
3 cups riced cauliflower

1. Press the Sauté button on the Instant Pot® and heat coconut oil. Add ground beef, onion, and parsnip; stir-fry 5 minutes until onions are tender and beef is almost all brown. Add garlic and pour in wine; heat 1 minute to allow the alcohol to burn off.

2. Add tomato paste, cumin, salt, oregano, green olives, capers, and caper juice to pot and stir to mix. Lock lid. Press the Manual or Pressure Cook button and adjust time to 0 minutes. When timer beeps, quick-release pressure until float valve drops and then unlock lid.

3. Transfer pot ingredients to a large bowl. Drain all but 2 tablespoons liquid from the pot. Add cauliflower to pot and heat 2–3 minutes until heated through.

4. Transfer cauliflower to serving bowls and top with beef mixture. Serve warm.

Chi-Town Italian Beef and Peppers

A giant bowl of beef and peppers will make you think you are in Chicago, strolling the Navy Pier, shopping the Magnificent Mile, or even at Portillo's enjoying your Italian Beef, minus the dipped bun!

- **Hands-On Time: 15 minutes**
- **Cook Time: 52 minutes**

Serves 6

2 tablespoons coconut oil

3 pounds chuck roast, halved

1 large onion, peeled, halved, and sliced

2 medium red bell peppers, seeded and sliced

2 medium green bell peppers, seeded and sliced

1 (16-ounce) jar sliced pepperoncini, including juice

3 cloves garlic, quartered

1 cup beef broth

1 teaspoon freshly ground black pepper

1 Press the Sauté button on the Instant Pot® and heat coconut oil until melted. Add roast and sear on all sides for a total of 12 minutes.

2 Add onion, bell peppers, pepperoncini, garlic, and beef broth to pot. Lock lid. Press the Manual or Pressure Cook button and adjust time for 40 minutes. When timer beeps, quick-release any remaining pressure until float valve drops and then unlock lid.

3 Transfer roast to a cutting board and let rest 10 minutes. Use a slotted spoon to transfer onions and peppers to a large bowl. Thinly slice roast and add to the bowl. Transfer a few small spoonfuls of pot liquid to the bowl. Toss with black pepper. Serve warm.

Beef Shanks and Artichokes

This quick dish is a succulent meal for two that can be accomplished in no time. The salty and smooth artichoke hearts couple brilliantly with the fresh tomatoes. On a side note, the heated lycopene in the tomatoes is especially beneficial to men, aiding in the protection against prostate cancer and erectile dysfunction.

- **Hands-On Time: 5 minutes**
- **Cook Time: 4 minutes**

Serves 2

2 (1"-thick) beef shanks (total 1½ pounds)

1 teaspoon sea salt

½ teaspoon freshly ground black pepper

1 tablespoon avocado oil

1 (14-ounce) can quartered artichoke hearts, including juice

10 grape tomatoes, halved

1 Season beef shanks on both sides with salt and pepper.

2 Press the Sauté button on the Instant Pot® and heat oil. Add beef shanks and sear 2 minutes per side.

3 Add remaining ingredients to pot. Lock lid. Press the Manual or Pressure Cook button and adjust time to 0 minutes. When timer beeps, quick-release pressure until float valve drops and then unlock lid.

4 Transfer beef to a cutting board and let rest 5 minutes.

5 Use a slotted spoon to transfer artichoke hearts and tomatoes to a bowl. Slice beef and serve with vegetables. Spoon over some of the pot juice if desired.

Bison Sloppy Joe's

Who needs a bun, when all the good stuff is in the sloppy?! Bison is such a lean meat alternative that is rich in iron, zinc, and vitamin B_{12}. And move over salmon, bison is also a great source of omega-3 fatty acids.

- **Hands-On Time: 10 minutes**
- **Cook Time: 4 minutes**

Serves 2

1 tablespoon avocado oil

1 pound ground bison

1 medium yellow onion, peeled and diced

1 small green bell pepper, seeded and diced

1 stalk celery, finely chopped

2 teaspoons Worcestershire sauce

2 cups tomato sauce

2 tablespoons tomato paste

1 tablespoon pure maple syrup

1 teaspoon sea salt

1 teaspoon freshly ground black pepper

1 Press the Sauté button on the Instant Pot® and heat oil. Add bison, onion, green pepper, and celery; stir-fry 3–4 minutes until onions are tender and bison is mostly browned.

2 Add remaining ingredients to pot. Lock lid. Press the Manual or Pressure Cook button and adjust time to 0 minutes. When timer beeps, quick-release pressure until float valve drops and then unlock lid.

3 Transfer mixture to serving bowls and serve warm.

Ground Bison Bulgogi

Bulgogi is conventionally made with thin strips of marinated beef, but in this quick recipe, ground bison is used utilizing all the flavors. Enjoy this Korean classic as a modern bowl of yum using a quick Western take on the tradition.

- **Hands-On Time: 10 minutes**
- **Cook Time: 5 minutes**

Serves 3

1 tablespoon sesame oil

1 pound ground bison

5 green onions, sliced (whites and greens separated)

1 small carrot, peeled and diced

3 cloves garlic, minced

¼ cup coconut aminos

2 tablespoons pure maple syrup

1 tablespoon apple cider vinegar

1 medium red apple, peeled, cored, and grated

1 teaspoon minced ginger

2 teaspoons toasted sesame seeds

1 Press the Sauté button on the Instant Pot® and heat oil. Add ground bison, onion whites, and carrot; stir-fry 3–4 minutes until onions are tender and bison is almost all brown. Add garlic and heat 1 additional minute.

2 Add coconut aminos, syrup, vinegar, apple, and ginger to pot and stir to mix. Lock lid. Press the Manual or Pressure Cook button and adjust time to 0 minutes. When timer beeps, quick-release pressure until float valve drops and then unlock lid.

3 Transfer pot ingredients to serving bowls. Garnish with sesame seeds and onion greens.

Italian Beef Tongue Lettuce Wraps

So, beef tongue is completely a mental game. For first-timers, having a giant tongue on your cutting board can be somewhat off-putting. Once you can get past your personal mind games, there is incredibly tasty and juicy meat hidden in a scary form, and it is ideal for lettuce wraps.

- **Hands-On Time: 15 minutes**
- **Cook Time: 43 minutes**

Serves 4

1½ pounds beef tongue

1 medium white onion, peeled and roughly diced

4 cloves garlic, halved

2 bay leaves

1 teaspoon ground cumin

1 teaspoon smoked paprika

1 teaspoon stone-ground mustard

1 teaspoon ground coriander

1 teaspoon celery seed

4 cups water

8 iceberg lettuce leaves

3 Roma tomatoes, seeded and diced

¼ cup julienned radishes

1 medium avocado, peeled and diced

1 medium lime, quartered

1 Place tongue, onion, garlic, bay leaves, cumin, smoked paprika, mustard, coriander, celery seed, and water in the Instant Pot®. Lock lid. Press the Manual or Pressure Cook button and adjust time to 40 minutes. When timer beeps, quick-release pressure until float valve drops and then unlock lid.

2 Transfer tongue to a cutting board and let rest until cool enough to handle. Make a shallow cut lengthwise down the center of the tongue. Peel off and discard the thick outer layer. Cut off and discard any gristle at the back of the tongue. Dice the tongue meat and return it to the pot juices. Let simmer 2–3 minutes.

3 Use a slotted spoon to transfer the meat to a bowl. Serve with lettuce leaves, tomatoes, radishes, avocado, and lime.

Pork, Lamb, and Game Main Dishes

From Salsa Verde Pulled Pork and a tasty Cubano Bowl to Osso Bucco with Gremolata and Greek Lamb Meatballs, this chapter will take you around the world with new flavors and spices. You may even be trying lamb or veal for the first time and this chapter will show you just how to season it. And the Instant Pot® is the perfect kitchen appliance to yield juicy cuts of meat with its high-pressure method of cooking. In addition, it is an essential tool in the summer because it doesn't emit excess heat as the oven does. Because of this quicker cooking time, you'll have that barbecue dish on the picnic table in no time, allowing you to concentrate on your family and friends without heating up the house.

Salsa Verde Pulled Pork

Of all the magic tricks that the Instant Pot® has up its proverbial sleeve, the grand act is the cooking of a pork shoulder and the amount of time it takes. What used to take many hours to yield tender pull-apart pork can now be done in less than 2 hours.

- **Hands-On Time: 15 minutes**
- **Cook Time: 95 minutes**

Serves 8

1 (5-pound) bone-in pork butt or shoulder

2 teaspoons sea salt

1 teaspoon freshly ground black pepper

4 cups beef broth

1 cup Salsa Verde (see Chapter 4)

1 Pat pork butt with paper towels and set aside. Season with salt and pepper.

2 Place the pork butt in the Instant Pot®. Add beef broth. Lock lid. Press the Manual or Pressure Cook button and adjust time to 85 minutes. When timer beeps, let pressure release naturally until float valve drops and then unlock lid. Check the pork to make sure it can easily pull apart. If not, press the Sauté button and simmer unlidded for an additional 10 minutes.

3 With the meat still in the Instant Pot®, use two forks and pull pork apart. Remove bone and discard. Use a slotted spoon to transfer the pork to a serving bowl. Toss in Salsa Verde and 2–3 tablespoons of broth from the pot. Serve warm.

Simple Dijon Pork Tenderloin

Pork tenderloin is a go-to for most busy home cooks, but overcooked, it can become dried out and become sad. With the Instant Pot®, the steam helps keep the moisture in the air around the loin while it is cooking. Enjoy this pork sliced into medallions alongside a simple salad or roasted vegetables.

- **Hands-On Time: 5 minutes**
- **Cook Time: 20 minutes**

Serves 4

2 (2-pound) loins, each halved

2 tablespoons whole-grain Dijon mustard

1 teaspoon sea salt

1 teaspoon freshly ground black pepper

1 cup water

3 cloves garlic, halved

1 Pat pork loins with paper towels. Massage with mustard. Season with salt and pepper.

2 Pour water into the Instant Pot®. Add garlic. Place loins on a steamer basket and insert in pot. Lock lid. Press the Manual or Pressure Cook button and adjust time to 20 minutes. When timer beeps, quick-release pressure until float valve drops and then unlock lid.

3 Transfer pork loins to a serving tray and either slice into medallions or pull apart pork with two forks. Serve warm.

Orange Rosemary Pork Tenderloin

Such a decadent cut of protein, tenderloins take on the flavors they are cooked with, lending a salty and fatty note. Combined with the citrus from the orange and the piney essence and earthiness from the rosemary, this dish is a winner.

- **Hands-On Time: 5 minutes**
- **Cook Time: 20 minutes**

Serves 4

- ⅓ cup freshly squeezed orange juice (about 1 orange)
- 1 tablespoon orange zest
- 1 tablespoon finely chopped rosemary
- 2 tablespoons honey
- 1 teaspoon sea salt
- ½ teaspoon freshly ground black pepper
- 2 (2-pound) loins, each halved
- ½ cup water

1 In large bowl, combine orange juice, orange zest, rosemary, honey, salt, and pepper. Add pork, toss, and refrigerate covered at least 30 minutes or up to overnight.

2 Place pork in the Instant Pot® and add remaining marinade. Add water. Lock lid. Press the Manual or Pressure Cook button and adjust time to 20 minutes. When timer beeps, quick-release pressure until float valve drops and then unlock lid.

3 Transfer pork loins to a serving tray and either slice into medallions or pull apart pork with two forks. Serve warm.

Balsamic Pork Tenderloin with Caperberries

The reduced balsamic sauce is such a rich and luxurious sweet flavor. Add the little salt bombs of caperberries to balance out the flavor. Caperberries are the fruit of the caper bush. They are usually brined and eaten or used in recipes as you would olives. The brininess is a wonderful complement to the balsamic vinegar.

- **Hands-On Time: 5 minutes**
- **Cook Time: 25 minutes**

Serves 4

2 (2-pound) loins, each halved
1 teaspoon sea salt
1 teaspoon freshly ground black pepper
4 tablespoons ghee, divided
½ cup beef broth
¼ cup balsamic vinegar
2 tablespoons caperberries, stems removed

1 Season pork with salt and pepper.

2 Press the Sauté button on the Instant Pot® and heat 2 tablespoons ghee. Sear loins on all sides for a total of about 4–5 minutes.

3 Add beef broth to pot. Lock lid. Press the Manual or Pressure Cook button and adjust time to 15 minutes. When timer beeps, quick-release pressure until float valve drops and then unlock lid. Transfer pork to a plate.

4 Add balsamic vinegar and remaining ghee to pot. Heat 4–5 minutes until sauce is reduced. Add caperberries and heat 1 additional minute.

5 Slice pork and serve warm with sauce and caperberries.

Steamed Dry-Rubbed Pork Spareribs

No sticky sauce needed here. These ribs will be as smooth as butter and have all the flavoring needed with the broad mix of simple spices.

- **Hands-On Time: 10 minutes**
- **Cook Time: 30 minutes**

Serves 6

1 rack pork ribs (about 3½ pounds)
1 teaspoon sea salt
1 teaspoon freshly ground black pepper
1 teaspoon smoked paprika
1 teaspoon chili powder
1 teaspoon garlic powder
1 teaspoon Italian seasoning
1 cup water

1 Cut ribs into 2-rib sections. In a large bowl, combine salt, pepper, paprika, chili powder, garlic powder, and Italian seasoning. Toss in rib sections to coat. Refrigerate covered at least 30 minutes or up to overnight.

2 Add water to the Instant Pot® and insert trivet or steamer basket. Arrange ribs standing upright with the meaty side facing outward. Lock lid. Press the Manual or Pressure Cook button and adjust time to 30 minutes. When timer beeps, let pressure release naturally until float valve drops and then unlock lid.

3 Transfer ribs to a platter and serve warm.

Cowgirl Baby Back Pork Ribs

These Instant Pot® ribs are amazingly juicy due to the pressure and constant steam in the pot. Don't skip the coffee crystals with this rustically charming recipe. It adds a beautiful earthiness to the ribs. If you want a little crispness to the ribs, throw them on the grill or under a broiler for a couple of minutes until browned on each side.

- **Hands-On Time: 10 minutes**
- **Cook Time: 25 minutes**

Serves 4

2 racks (about 3 pounds) baby back pork ribs
1 teaspoon instant coffee crystals
1 teaspoon sea salt
½ teaspoon chili powder
½ teaspoon ground cumin
½ teaspoon cayenne pepper
½ teaspoon stone-ground mustard
½ teaspoon garlic powder
½ teaspoon onion powder
¼ teaspoon ground coriander
1 medium onion, peeled and diced
4 cloves garlic, halved
2 cups water

1 Cut ribs into 2-rib sections. In a large bowl, combine coffee, salt, chili powder, cumin, cayenne pepper, mustard, garlic powder, onion powder, and coriander. Toss in rib sections to coat. Refrigerate covered at least 30 minutes or up to overnight.

2 Place onions, garlic, and water in the Instant Pot® and insert trivet. Arrange ribs standing upright with the meaty side facing outward. Lock lid. Press the Manual or Pressure Cook button and adjust time to 25 minutes. When timer beeps, let pressure release naturally until float valve drops and then unlock lid.

3 Transfer ribs to a platter and serve warm.

WHAT ARE AROMATICS?
Even though the onion and garlic are not part of the actual final meal in this recipe, the fragrance created in the steam adds another level of flavor due to the aroma from the onion and garlic.

Ham and Scalloped Potatoes

When you are just craving some TV-binge time and needing a little comfort food, grab your remote and a blanket and cozy up to this bowl of salty, creamy, decadent delight.

- **Hands-On Time: 10 minutes**
- **Cook Time: 15 minutes**

Serves 4

4 tablespoons ghee, divided

½ medium yellow onion, peeled and sliced into half-moons

1 teaspoon sea salt

½ teaspoon freshly ground black pepper

⅓ cup unsweetened almond milk

1 teaspoon cassava flour

3 small russet potatoes, thinly sliced

1 cup diced ham

1 Press the Sauté button on the Instant Pot® and heat 3 tablespoons ghee. Add onion and stir-fry 2–3 minutes until tender. Add salt, pepper, and milk. Whisk in flour. Press the Cancel button.

2 Lightly grease a 7-cup glass bowl and layer ⅓ of potatoes in the dish. Add ⅓ of the ham. Add ⅓ of the onion mixture. Repeat two more times until you have three layers. Top with remaining ghee.

3 Place trivet in Instant Pot® and place the glass bowl on top. Lock lid. Press the Manual or Pressure Cook button and adjust time to 12 minutes. When timer beeps, quick-release pressure until float valve drops and then unlock lid.

4 Remove dish from pot and serve warm.

Ground Pork Stir-Fry Bowl

Forget about take-out food full of MSG, soy, and bad fats. Make your own quick and healthy version of Chinese take-out. Heck, you can even buy those great take-out boxes and wooden chopsticks if you miss the feel of holding the box while binge-watching the latest and greatest series.

- **Hands-On Time: 10 minutes**
- **Cook Time: 7 minutes**

Serves 4

2 teaspoons sesame oil

1 pound ground pork

½ medium yellow onion, peeled and diced

¼ cup coconut aminos

¼ cup water

1 teaspoon Chinese five spice powder

1 cup sliced shiitake mushrooms

¼ cup peeled and julienned carrots

1 overflowing cup chopped fresh kale

WHAT IS CHINESE FIVE SPICE?
Although there are a few variations, Chinese five spice is traditionally a blend of star anise, cloves, cinnamon, Szechuan peppers, and fennel seeds. It can be found already combined in the spice section of most grocery stores.

1 Press the Sauté button on the Instant Pot® and heat oil. Add pork and onion; stir-fry 4 minutes until pork starts to brown.

2 Add coconut aminos, water, Chinese spice, mushrooms, and carrots. Lock lid. Press the Manual or Pressure Cook button and adjust time to 3 minutes. When timer beeps, quick-release pressure until float valve drops and then unlock lid.

3 Add kale to the pot and toss until it begins to wilt. Transfer to serving bowls. Serve warm.

Smothered Pork Chops with Mushroom Gravy

This is a classic country-style dish for a reason. It just hits all the right comfort buttons. Add some mashed cauliflower to round out this meal.

- **Hands-On Time: 10 minutes**
- **Cook Time: 25 minutes**

Serves 4

2 tablespoons avocado oil

4 (1"-thick) bone-in pork chops

1 teaspoon sea salt

½ teaspoon freshly ground black pepper

1 cup beef broth

3 cups sliced baby bella or cremini mushrooms

1 small Vidalia onion, peeled and sliced into half-moons

2 tablespoons unsweetened almond milk

2 teaspoons Worcestershire sauce

2 tablespoons arrowroot flour

1 Press the Sauté button on the Instant Pot®. Heat oil. Season pork chops with salt and pepper. Sear chops 2–3 minutes per side in batches. Set pork aside.

2 Add broth, mushrooms, and onion to the pot. Insert steamer basket. Add pork chops, propping them up on the sides so as not to overlap. Lock lid. Press the Manual or Pressure Cook button and adjust time to 15 minutes. When timer beeps, let pressure release naturally for 5 minutes. Quick-release any remaining pressure until float valve drops and then unlock lid.

3 Remove pork chops and steamer basket. Add milk and Worcestershire sauce to pot with juices and broth. Slowly whisk in flour, 1 teaspoon a time, until a gravy forms. Transfer mushroom gravy to a bowl and serve with pork chops. Season with more salt if desired.

Pork Chops with Sauerkraut, Potatoes, and Apples

These pork chops are juicy and flavorful with a German flair from the addition of beer, potatoes, sauerkraut, and caraway seeds. If you're looking for a nonalcoholic option, feel free to substitute beef broth for the beer.

- **Hands-On Time: 15 minutes**
- **Cook Time: 30 minutes**

Serves 4

2 tablespoons avocado oil

4 (1"-thick) bone-in pork chops

1 teaspoon sea salt

½ teaspoon freshly ground black pepper

4 slices bacon, diced

1 stalk celery, finely chopped

3 large carrots, peeled and sliced

1 large yellow onion, peeled and diced

1 clove garlic, minced

1 (12-ounce) bottle gluten-free beer

4 medium red potatoes, peeled and quartered

2 medium red apples, peeled, cored, and quartered

1 (1-pound) bag high-quality sauerkraut, rinsed and drained

1 tablespoon caraway seeds

1 Press the Sauté button on the Instant Pot®. Heat oil. Season pork chops with salt and pepper. In batches, sear pork chops 2–3 minutes per side. Set pork aside.

2 Add bacon, celery, carrots, and onion to the pot. Stir-fry 3–5 minutes until the onions are translucent. Add garlic and cook 1 minute. Add beer and deglaze the pot by stirring and scraping the bottom and sides to loosen any browned bits. Simmer unlidded for 5 minutes.

3 Add potatoes, apples, and sauerkraut. Sprinkle with caraway seeds. Slightly prop pork chops up against the sides of the pot so as not to crowd the pork. Lock lid. Press the Manual or Pressure Cook button and adjust time to 15 minutes. When timer beeps, let pressure release naturally for 5 minutes. Quick-release any remaining pressure until float valve drops and then unlock lid.

4 Transfer the pork chops, sauerkraut, potatoes, and apples to a serving dish. Serve warm.

Cubano Bowl

You'll never miss the bread from the traditional Cubano sandwich with this recipe. You still get the tender pork, ham, mustard, and pickles. Although there is no Swiss cheese in this recipe, the nutritional yeast fulfills that note of nuttiness and "cheese."

- **Hands-On Time: 15 minutes**
- **Cook Time: 95 minutes**

Serves 8

1 (5-pound) bone-in pork butt or shoulder

1½ teaspoons sea salt, divided

1½ teaspoons freshly ground black pepper, divided

½ medium yellow onion, peeled and chopped

1 cup water

1 tablespoon fresh lime juice

1 tablespoon fresh orange juice

1 teaspoon garlic powder

1 teaspoon dried oregano

1 teaspoon cayenne pepper

2 teaspoons ground cumin

1 tablespoon nutritional yeast

2 cups diced smoked ham

1 cup diced dill pickles

8 teaspoons yellow mustard

1 Dry pork butt with paper towels. Season with ½ teaspoon salt and pepper. Set aside.

2 Place the pork butt in the Instant Pot®. Add onion, water, lime juice, orange juice, garlic powder, oregano, cayenne pepper, cumin, nutritional yeast, and remaining salt and pepper.

3 Press the Manual or Pressure Cook button and adjust time to 85 minutes. When timer beeps, let pressure release naturally until float valve drops and then unlock lid. Check the pork to make sure it can easily pull apart. If not, press the Sauté button and simmer unlidded an additional 10 minutes.

4 Use two forks to shred the pork in the pot. Remove the bone and discard. Use a slotted spoon to transfer the pork to separate bowls. Garnish with ham, pickles, and a drizzle of yellow mustard.

Vietnamese Pork Chops

This unique twist of sweet and spicy flavors complements the saltiness of the pork so well. There are just enough red chili pepper flakes to balance out the flavors of this dish, but if heat is your thing, go for it and add some more!

- **Hands-On Time: 10 minutes**
- **Cook Time: 15 minutes**

Serves 4

Marinade

2 ripe plums, pitted
1 small bunch cilantro, including stems
2 tablespoons molasses
2 tablespoons fresh lime juice
1 teaspoon lime zest
Pinch dried red pepper flakes
3 cloves garlic, minced
½" piece fresh garlic, peeled and minced
¼ cup avocado oil
1 teaspoon sea salt

Pork Chops

4 (1"-thick) bone-in pork chops
1 cup water

1   In a food processor, combine all marinade ingredients and pulse until smooth. Transfer to a large bowl, add pork chops and toss. Marinate covered or sealed in the refrigerator at least 1 hour or up to overnight.

2   Add water to the Instant Pot® and insert steamer basket. Add pork chops to steamer basket. Pour excess marinade over pork chops. Lock lid. Press the Manual or Pressure Cook button and adjust time to 15 minutes. When timer beeps, let pressure release naturally for 5 minutes. Quick-release any remaining pressure until float valve drops and then unlock lid.

3   Transfer the pork chops to a serving tray. Serve warm.

BBQ Boneless Pork Loin Roast

The boneless loin roast is a center cut of pork. It is not the tenderloin and it is not the shoulder. Be aware of the different cuts as they will have different cooking times and results. For instance, pork shoulder or butt is perfect for shredding for barbecue dishes and takes longer to prepare. Pork tenderloin is more narrow and long and requires a lower cooking time.

- **Hands-On Time: 10 minutes**
- **Cook Time: 41 minutes**

Serves 6

Roast
2 teaspoons sea salt
1 teaspoon freshly ground black pepper
1 teaspoon garlic powder
2½ pounds boneless pork loin roast
2 cups water

Barbecue Sauce
¼ cup water
¾ cup paleo ketchup
½ medium onion, peeled and grated
¼ cup molasses
1 teaspoon garlic powder
1 teaspoon ground cumin
¼ teaspoon cayenne pepper
1 tablespoon yellow mustard
2 teaspoons apple cider vinegar

1 In a small bowl, mix together salt, pepper, and garlic powder. Massage into roast.

2 Add water to the Instant Pot®. Add roast. Lock lid. Press the Manual or Pressure Cook button and adjust for 30 minutes. When timer beeps, let pressure release naturally for 10 minutes. Quick-release any remaining pressure until float valve drops and then unlock lid.

3 Transfer loin to a plate. Discard liquid from pot. Add barbecue sauce ingredients. Press the Sauté button. Stir and sauté 4–5 minutes until sauce starts to reduce and thicken. Ladle out ½ cup sauce and set aside.

4 Return pork to pot and sauté 6 minutes, turning roast until all sides are covered and sauce is caramelized. Transfer roast to a cutting board. Let rest 5 minutes.

5 Thinly slice roast and pour reserved sauce over slices. Serve warm.

Osso Bucco with Gremolata

Fall off the bone, hearty, and flavorful are just a few ways to describe this scrumptious meal. And don't forget about that bone marrow. To. Die. For. The gremolata just freshens everything up. Add two more shanks for an extraordinary dinner party experience with your favorite couple.

- **Hands-On Time: 15 minutes**
- **Cook Time: 41 minutes**

Serves 2

Gremolata

⅓ cup chopped fresh Italian flat-leaf parsley

2 teaspoons lemon zest

2 cloves garlic, minced

Osso Bucco

2 (1½") bone-in veal shanks (about 3¼ pounds total weight)

1 teaspoon sea salt

1 teaspoon freshly ground black pepper

1 tablespoon avocado oil

1 (28-ounce) can crushed tomatoes, including juice

1 In a small bowl, combine gremolata ingredients and refrigerate covered until ready to use.

2 Season both sides of veal shanks with salt and pepper.

3 Press the Sauté button on the Instant Pot® and heat oil. Sear veal shanks about 3 minutes per side until browned.

4 Add crushed tomatoes, including juice. Lock lid. Press the Meat/Stew button and adjust time to 35 minutes. When timer beeps, quick-release pressure until float valve drops and then unlock lid.

5 Transfer Osso Bucco and tomato sauce to two shallow bowls. Garnish with gremolata. Serve warm.

Pork Medallions Puttanesca

With just the right fat and salt from the pork married to this lusty derivative-named sauce, there is no way this quick dish won't be a home run with a date night with your sweetie.

- **Hands-On Time: 10 minutes**
- **Cook Time: 12 minutes**

Serves 4

2-pound pork tenderloin, cut into 1" rounds

1 teaspoon salt

½ teaspoon freshly ground black pepper

2 tablespoons avocado oil, divided

1½ cups Puttanesca Sauce (see Chapter 4)

2 tablespoons water

1. Season pork medallions with salt and pepper on both sides. Set aside.

2. Press the Sauté button on the Instant Pot® and heat 1 tablespoon oil. Sear half the pork 1 minute on each side. Set aside. Repeat with remaining oil and pork.

3. Add Puttanesca Sauce and water to pot. Gently toss in pork medallions. Lock lid. Press the Manual or Pressure Cook button and adjust time to 8 minutes. When timer beeps, quick-release pressure until float valve drops and then unlock lid.

4. Transfer pork medallions and sauce to a dish and serve warm.

Lamb Riblets

These little riblets are so tasty that there is no need to douse them in a thick barbecue sauce. Sweet and simple helps enhance the natural flavor. Smaller than traditional beef or pork ribs, these also make a great finger food for guests.

- **Hands-On Time: 5 minutes**
- **Cook Time: 15 minutes**

Serves 2

½ teaspoon sea salt

½ teaspoon garlic salt

1 teaspoon smoked paprika

1½ pounds lamb riblets

2 tablespoons avocado oil

1 (14.5-ounce) can crushed fire-roasted tomatoes, including juice

1. In a small bowl, combine sea salt, garlic salt, and paprika. Massage into lamb riblets.

2. Press the Sauté button on the Instant Pot® and heat oil. Add riblets and sear on each side for a total of 4–5 minutes. Add tomatoes, including juice. Lock lid. Press the Manual or Pressure Cook button and adjust time to 10 minutes. When timer beeps, let pressure release naturally for 10 minutes. Quick-release any remaining pressure until float valve drops and then unlock lid.

3. Transfer ribs to a plate and serve warm.

Lamb Shanks with Tomato Curry Sauce

Lamb shanks are an amazing protein that easily take on the flavors they are cooked with. That's why the Tomato Curry Sauce is a spectacular sauce to pair with these meaty shanks.

- **Hands-On Time: 10 minutes**
- **Cook Time: 40 minutes**

Serves 2

2 bone-in lamb shanks (about 1½ pounds)
1 teaspoon sea salt
½ teaspoon freshly ground black pepper
¼ cup ghee
2 medium carrots, peeled and cut into ½" pieces
2 cups Tomato Curry Sauce (see Chapter 4)
1 cup water
¼ cup chopped fresh cilantro

1 Season both sides of veal shanks with salt and pepper.

2 Press the Sauté button on the Instant Pot® and heat ghee. Sear veal shanks 2–3 minutes per side until browned.

3 Add carrots, tomato curry sauce, and water to pot. Toss ingredients. Lock lid. Press the Meat/Stew button and adjust time to 35 minutes. When timer beeps, quick-release pressure until float valve drops and then unlock lid.

4 Transfer shanks, tomato curry sauce, and carrots to two shallow bowls. Garnish with cilantro. Serve warm.

Greek Lamb Meatballs

Called *keftedes* in Greece, let these meatballs take you on a temporary vacation to the Mediterranean. Serve as is, on a salad, or with some traditional tzatziki sauce.

- **Hands-On Time: 15 minutes**
- **Cook Time: 11 minutes**

Yields 16 meatballs

1 pound ground lamb
1 large egg
½ teaspoon lemon zest
½ cup chopped fresh mint
¼ cup almond meal
2 tablespoons finely diced red onion
½ teaspoon ground coriander
½ teaspoon ground cumin
Pinch ground cinnamon
Pinch ground nutmeg
1 teaspoon sea salt
2 tablespoons avocado oil, divided
½ cup water
1 large lemon, cut into 6 wedges
1 tablespoon chopped fresh dill

1 In a medium bowl, combine lamb, egg, lemon zest, mint, almond meal, diced onion, coriander, cumin, cinnamon, nutmeg, and salt. Form into 16 golf ball–sized meatballs. Set aside.

2 Press the Sauté button on the Instant Pot® and heat 1 tablespoon oil. Place 8 meatballs around the edges of the pot. Sear all sides of the meatballs for a total of about 4 minutes. Remove the first batch and set aside. Add remaining oil and meatballs and sear 4 minutes. Remove meatballs.

3 Add water to the Instant Pot® and insert steamer basket. Place meatballs evenly on steamer basket. Lock lid. Press the Manual or Pressure Cook button and adjust time to 3 minutes. When timer beeps, quick-release pressure until float valve drops and then unlock lid.

4 Transfer meatballs to a serving plate and garnish with lemon wedges and fresh dill.

TZATZIKI SAUCE AND HOW TO MAKE IT
Tzatziki is a yogurt-based sauce served with grilled meats. If you allow yogurt into your diet, this sauce pairs exquisitely with these Greek Lamb Meatballs. To make a quick sauce, combine the following ingredients and then refrigerate lidded until use: 8-ounces plain Greek yogurt, 1 medium peeled, seeded, and diced cucumber, 1 tablespoon olive oil, 1 teaspoon lemon juice, 2 minced cloves of garlic, 2 teaspoons chopped fresh dill. Season with salt and pepper to taste.

Chorizo Sliders with Jicama-Beet Slaw

These Chorizo Sliders with Jicama-Beet Slaw yield the heat from the chorizo and coolness from the slaw to create an undeniably nomtastic combination!

- **Hands-On Time: 15 minutes**
- **Cook Time: 10 minutes**

Serves 4

Jicama-Beet Slaw
1 cup grated jicama
½ cup peeled and grated beets
⅛ cup freshly squeezed orange juice
1 tablespoon olive oil
½ teaspoon chopped dill
Pinch sea salt

Sliders
½ pound ground chorizo
½ pound ground pork
2 tablespoons seeded and finely diced green pepper
1 teaspoon smoked paprika
2 tablespoons coconut oil, divided
1 cup water

Garnish
1 medium avocado, peeled and sliced
8 tomato slices

1. In a medium bowl, combine slaw ingredients. Refrigerate until ready to use.

2. In a large bowl, combine ground chorizo, pork, green pepper, and paprika. Form into 8 slider patties. Set aside.

3. Press the Sauté button on the Instant Pot® and heat 1 tablespoon oil. Place 4 patties in the pot. Sear each side of the burgers 2 minutes each side. Remove the patties and set aside. Add another tablespoon of oil and remaining patties and sear them. Set aside.

4. Add water to the Instant Pot®. Add steamer basket. Prop patties evenly on steamer basket. Lock lid. Press the Manual or Pressure Cook button and adjust time to 2 minutes. When timer beeps, quick-release pressure until float valve drops and then unlock lid.

5. Transfer slider patties to plate. Serve warm with avocado and tomato slices. Dollop slaw on top of each slider.

The Busy Cook's Duck à l'Orange Breast

Your dinner mate will think you studied for years at Le Cordon Bleu when serving this French classic dish, when in actuality, it only took you about 20 minutes tops to get this to a plate. Bon appétit!

- **Hands-On Time: 10 minutes**
- **Cook Time: 10 minutes**

Serves 2

⅓ cup freshly squeezed orange juice (about 1 orange)

1 tablespoon orange zest

2 tablespoons honey

1 pound duck breasts (about 2–3 breasts)

1 teaspoon sea salt

½ teaspoon freshly ground black pepper

2 teaspoons cassava flour

1 In a small bowl, whisk together orange juice, orange zest, and honey.

2 Season both sides of duck breasts with salt and pepper. Carefully score the duck fat in a cross-hatch pattern making sure to avoid the meat.

3 Press the Sauté button on the Instant Pot® and place duck breasts fat side down. Heat 8 minutes. Do not touch the duck as it is rendering off its fat. After 8 minutes, remove duck to a plate. Pour out all fat except for 1 teaspoon. Add duck back to the pot with the fat side up. Add orange juice mixture. Lock lid. Press the Manual or Pressure Cook button and adjust time to 2 minutes. Adjust the pressure to Low. When timer beeps, quick-release pressure until float valve drops and then unlock lid.

4 Transfer duck to a cutting board and let rest 5 minutes. Whisk flour into pot juices until thickened.

5 Slice duck and transfer to plates. Drizzle sauce from pot over duck. Serve warm.

9

Seafood and Fish Main Dishes

Seafood is one of those meals that gets ordered a lot at restaurants but gets overlooked at home. Seafood is a great paleo source of protein and is something to embrace. A lot of home chefs are timid when it comes to cooking fish and shellfish but that's a shame. Fish and shellfish are not only low in calories and full of nutrients, but they are some of the quickest meals you can cook in your Instant Pot®. In addition, the steaming functionality of the appliance makes for some tender and moist meals.

If you are purchasing fresh seafood rather than sealed, frozen seafood, make sure it comes from a trusted source. Don't be afraid to ask when the shipment came in, where it came from, if it was wild-caught, and whether or not the fishmonger can prepare the fish for you. If that fishmonger can't or won't answer those questions, find another one. Once you have made your choice, prepare your meal within 1–2 days for optimal freshness.

The Instant Pot® can easily and perfectly cook your seafood with its steam and pressure capabilities. The recipes in this chapter call for short cooking times and quick pressure release. You don't want to do a natural release with most fish as it will continue to cook if the pressure releases slowly. From a Fish Taco Bowl to Greek Sea Bass, this chapter covers a variety of recipes that will have you eating seafood on a regular basis.

Steamed Mussels and Chorizo

Mussels should be on the rotation of every family. They are inexpensive, quick to cook, and tasty. These nutrient-dense bivalves also pack a hefty dose of goodness such as omega-3 fatty acids, vitamin A, folate, and B_{12} as well as minerals such as phosphorus, zinc, and manganese.

- **Hands-On Time: 10 minutes**
- **Cook Time: 6 minutes**

Serves 4

2 tablespoons ghee

1 medium yellow onion, peeled and diced

½ pound chorizo, loose or cut from casings

3 cloves garlic, minced

1 (14.5-ounce) can diced tomatoes, including juice

½ teaspoon sea salt

2 pounds fresh mussels, cleaned and debearded

¼ cup chopped fresh Italian flat-leaf parsley

1 medium lemon, quartered

1 Press the Sauté button on the Instant Pot®. Add ghee and heat until melted. Add onion and chorizo and sauté 3 minutes. Add garlic and cook 1 additional minute. Stir in diced tomatoes, including juice, and salt. Cook an additional 2 minutes.

2 Add mussels. Lock lid. Press the Manual or Pressure Cook button and adjust time to 0 minutes. When timer beeps, quick-release pressure until float valve drops and then unlock lid.

3 Remove mussels and discard any that haven't opened. Transfer mussels to four bowls and pour chorizo mixture from Instant Pot® equally among bowls. Garnish each bowl with 1 tablespoon parsley and a lemon quarter. Serve immediately.

Stewed Halibut

Just for the halibut, eh? Rich in vitamins B_6 and B_{12}, potassium, and omega-3 fatty acids, this fish is a low calorie choice and mild tasting white flaky fish. Coupled with the tomatoes and other Mediterranean flavors, grab a glass of white wine while the Instant Pot® does your cooking.

- **Hands-On Time: 5 minutes**
- **Cook Time: 3 minutes**

Serves 2

1 (14.5-ounce) can diced tomatoes, including juice

½ cup chicken broth

¼ teaspoon onion powder

3 cloves garlic, minced

2 teaspoons smoked paprika

1 tablespoon chopped fresh tarragon

1 medium green bell pepper, seeded and small-diced

1 stalk celery, finely diced

1 teaspoon sea salt

¼ teaspoon freshly ground black pepper

1 pound halibut fillets, cut into bite-sized pieces

1 Add all ingredients except halibut to the Instant Pot® and stir to mix. Once mixed, add the fish on top. Lock lid. Press the Manual or Pressure Cook button and adjust time to 3 minutes. When timer beeps, quick-release pressure until float valve drops and then unlock lid.

2 Transfer all ingredients to a serving bowl. Serve warm.

Fish Taco Bowl

This recipe looks complicated, but you probably have most of the spices on hand. You can make the slaw and aioli ahead of time. Also, instead of grating your own cabbage and peeling a carrot, pick up a bag of coleslaw mix; it's the same thing. There is also broccoli slaw available for a twist. But do give this recipe a try. The variety of flavors will win your heart.

- **Hands-On Time: 15 minutes**
- **Cook Time: 3 minutes**

Serves 4

Slaw
½ cup grated green cabbage
1 large carrot, peeled and grated
Juice of ½ large lime
2 dashes sriracha
¼ cup chopped fresh cilantro
½ teaspoon sea salt

Spicy Aioli
¼ cup mayonnaise
Pinch salt
Squeeze lime juice
Dash sriracha

Fish
3 (6-ounce) cod fillets
Juice from ½ large lime
2 tablespoons fresh orange juice
1 teaspoon garlic salt
1 teaspoon ground cumin
1 tablespoon olive oil
1 cup water

Garnishes
1 medium avocado, peeled and diced
2 Roma tomatoes, seeded and diced
4 lime wedges

1 Combine slaw ingredients in a medium bowl. Refrigerate covered until ready to use.

2 Combine Spicy Aioli ingredients in a small bowl. Taste and adjust to your liking.

3 In a large bowl, combine fish, lime juice, orange juice, garlic salt, cumin, and olive oil and refrigerate 15 minutes.

4 Add 1 cup water to the Instant Pot® and insert trivet. Place steamer basket on top of trivet. Add cod in an even row onto steamer basket. Pour in marinade for the steaming aromatics. Lock lid. Press the Manual or Pressure Cook button and adjust time to 3 minutes. When timer beeps, quick-release pressure until float valve drops and then unlock lid.

5 Distribute slaw into serving bowls. Add fish and garnishes. Drizzle with aioli. Serve warm.

Thai Coconut Curry Monkfish

Known as the poor man's lobster, monkfish is a buttery and firm-textured whitefish that is unique and exquisite. Monkfish are certainly ugly, freaky looking sea creatures, but their taste is amazing. I suppose they represent the old adage, "Never trust a book by its cover." If so, no one would have ever put this guy on the grill.

- **Hands-On Time: 5 minutes**
- **Cook Time: 3 minutes**

Serves 4

1 (13.5-ounce) can coconut milk
Juice of 1 medium lime
1 tablespoon red curry paste
1 teaspoon fish sauce
1 teaspoon coconut aminos
1 teaspoon honey
2 teaspoons sriracha
2 cloves garlic, minced
1 teaspoon turmeric powder
1 teaspoon ground ginger
½ teaspoon sea salt
½ teaspoon white pepper
1 pound monkfish, cut into 1" cubes
¼ cup chopped fresh cilantro
3 lime wedges

1 In a large bowl, whisk together coconut milk, lime juice, red curry paste, fish sauce, coconut aminos, honey, sriracha, garlic, turmeric, ginger, sea salt, and white pepper.

2 Place monkfish in the bottom of the Instant Pot®. Pour coconut milk mixture over the fish. Lock lid. Press the Manual or Pressure Cook button and adjust time to 3 minutes. When timer beeps, quick-release pressure until float valve drops and then unlock lid.

3 Transfer fish and broth evenly into bowls. Garnish each with equal amounts of chopped cilantro and a lime wedge. Serve.

Louisiana Shrimp and Sausage

Eat this as is or served over a bed of riced cauliflower. Creole seasoning is a somewhat vague ingredient on this recipe list. Look in your local grocer's spice aisle and there will be several versions. Choose the one that speaks to you as you just can't go wrong with these beautiful spice blends.

- **Hands-On Time: 10 minutes**
- **Cook Time: 9 minutes**

Serves 4

2 tablespoons avocado oil

1 small onion, peeled and diced

1 stalk celery, diced

1 small green bell pepper, seeded and diced

1 (15-ounce) can diced tomatoes, including juice

1 tablespoon tomato paste

1 teaspoon honey

Pinch dried basil

2 teaspoons Creole seasoning

12 ounces fully cooked andouille sausage, sliced

1 pound large shrimp, peeled and deveined

½ teaspoon sea salt

¼ teaspoon freshly ground black pepper

1. Press the Sauté button on the Instant Pot® and heat oil. Add onion, celery, and bell pepper; sauté 3–5 minutes until onions are translucent and peppers are tender.

2. Stir in tomatoes and their juice, tomato paste, honey, basil, Creole seasoning, and sausage. Add shrimp. Lock lid. Press the Manual or Pressure Cook button and adjust time to 4 minutes. When timer beeps, quick-release pressure until float valve drops and then unlock lid.

3. Spoon into bowls, season with salt and pepper, and serve warm.

Shrimp, Prosciutto, and Asparagus Salad with Yuzu Vinaigrette

Yuzu kosho is the latest and greatest seasoning. It is citrusy and vinegary with a little kick, and chefs from around the globe are flocking to it. Yuzu is actually a Japanese fruit also known as citrus junos. To make a kosho paste, chefs use the peel from the yuzu and add chili pepper and salt. This mixture is then turned into a hot sauce.

- Hands-On Time: 5 minutes
- Cook Time: 0 minutes

Serves 2

Yuzu Vinaigrette
1 teaspoon yuzu kosho hot sauce
1 teaspoon honey
¼ cup extra-virgin olive oil
1 teaspoon apple cider vinegar
Pinch sea salt

Shrimp and Asparagus
1 cup water
1 bunch asparagus, cut into 1" pieces (woody ends removed)
1 teaspoon sea salt, divided
1 pound medium shrimp, peeled and deveined
Juice of ½ medium lemon
2 tablespoons ghee

Salad
2 overflowing cups of mixed greens
1 medium mango, peeled and diced
2 ounces prosciutto, ripped into pieces

1 In a small bowl, combine all vinaigrette ingredients. Set aside.

2 Add water to the Instant Pot® and insert trivet. Place steamer basket on trivet. Spread out the asparagus evenly over the bottom of the steamer basket. Sprinkle with ½ teaspoon salt. Add the shrimp, drizzle with lemon juice, and sprinkle with remaining ½ teaspoon salt. Place ghee evenly on top of shrimp in small scoops. Lock lid. Press the Steam button and adjust time to 0 minutes. When timer beeps, quick-release pressure until float valve drops and then unlock lid.

3 Place mixed greens in two serving bowls and toss with preferred amount of vinaigrette. Garnish with mango and prosciutto. Add steamed shrimp and asparagus. Serve.

Shrimp Scampi

Don't forget to mark your calendar for April 29, which is officially National Shrimp Scampi Day! Serve this as is or enjoy it over a bed of zoodled zucchini. After removing the shrimp from the Instant Pot®, put your vegetable "noodles" in the pot and heat in the same liquid 2–3 minutes until tender. Drain and serve with the shrimp on top. One pot cooking at its finest!

- **Hands-On Time: 5 minutes**
- **Cook Time: 8 minutes**

Serves 4

¼ cup ghee

6 cloves garlic, minced

½ cup dry white wine

1 medium lemon, halved

2 pounds large shrimp, peeled and deveined (tails on)

½ teaspoon sea salt

1 teaspoon lemon zest

¼ cup chopped fresh Italian flat-leaf parsley

1 Press the Sauté button on the Instant Pot®. Heat ghee and add garlic. Sauté 1–2 minutes until garlic starts to brown. Add wine and juice from ½ lemon. Continue to cook 2–3 minutes to allow alcohol to burn off.

2 Add shrimp to pot. Lock lid. Press the Steam button and adjust time to 3 minutes. When timer beeps, quick-release pressure until float valve drops and then unlock lid.

3 Spoon shrimp into bowls. Give a quick squeeze of the lemon over shrimp, and add salt and lemon zest. Garnish with parsley. Serve warm.

Crab-Chorizo Stuffed Calamari

There is more to calamari than just cutting them into little rings and deep-frying them. The bodies of calamari make the perfect little sausage casings and absolutely add more flavor. If you don't like the heat, substitute the spicy chorizo sausage for either ground pork or some mild Italian sausage. The result will still be unique and tasty!

- **Hands-On Time: 15 minutes**
- **Cook Time: 5 minutes**

Serves 4

Calamari

10–12 calamari tubes

¼ pound chorizo, loose or cut from casings

¼ cup crabmeat

1 large egg

1 tablespoon almond meal

Pinch sea salt

1 tablespoon finely diced shallot

1 cup water

Sauce

1 (14.5-ounce) can crushed tomatoes, including juice

2 teaspoons honey

3 cloves garlic, minced

½ teaspoon sea salt

2 tablespoons chopped chives

1 Rinse calamari tubes and set aside. In a medium bowl, combine chorizo, crab, egg, almond meal, salt, and diced shallot. Transfer mixture to a piping bag or plastic bag. Cut the tip off large enough for the mixture to pass through. Pipe sausage into calamari tubes. Fasten opening with a toothpick.

2 Add water to the Instant Pot® and insert steamer basket. Place stuffed calamari in an even row on steamer basket. Lock lid. Press the Manual or Pressure Cook button and adjust time to 3 minutes. When timer beeps, quick-release pressure until float valve drops and then unlock lid.

3 Remove steamer basket with the calamari from the pot and discard liquid. Add crushed tomatoes and juice to the Instant Pot®. Stir in honey, garlic, and salt. Add stuffed calamari. Sauté 2–3 minutes until sauce is warmed through and the internal temperature of the stuffed calamari reaches at least 160°F.

4 Remove toothpicks. Garnish with chives. Serve warm as a main course or as an appetizer.

Berbere Salmon

Berbere is an Ethiopian spice and herb blend that is a little fiery and a lot aromatic, which makes it a perfect romantic meal for two. It can be found in specialty spice shops or easily online. There are also several "make your own" recipes online. This spice blend is great on almost any protein.

- **Hands-On Time: 5 minutes**
- **Cook Time: 2 minutes**

Serves 2

2 (5-ounce) salmon fillets
1 tablespoon berbere seasoning
1 cup water
2 lemon wedges

1. Season salmon with berbere on all sides.

2. Pour water into the Instant Pot® and insert steamer basket. Place salmon on steamer basket. Lock lid. Press the Steam button and adjust time to 2 minutes. When timer beeps, quick-release pressure until float valve drops and then unlock lid.

3. Transfer fish to plates with lemon wedges. Serve immediately.

Dilled Salmon and Broccoli

Known for its beneficial omega-3 fatty acids, salmon is also high in vitamin B_{12}, vitamin D, and selenium, among others. Do your body good and quickly steam this very mild and flaky fish in the Instant Pot®. Adding the broccoli not only gives you more nutrients, but it makes this a complete meal with minimal cleanup.

- **Hands-On Time: 5 minutes**
- **Cook Time: 5 minutes**

Serves 2

2 (6-ounce) salmon fillets
½ teaspoon sea salt
4 lemon slices
2 teaspoons chopped fresh dill
1 cup water
1 small head broccoli, cut into florets

1. Pat fillets dry with a paper towel. Season salmon with salt. Place 2 lemon slices on each fillet. Sprinkle with chopped dill.

2. Add water to the Instant Pot® and insert steamer basket. Place salmon on steamer basket and scatter broccoli florets around the fillets. Lock lid. Press the Manual or Pressure Cook button and adjust time to 5 minutes. When timer beeps, quick-release pressure until float valve drops and then unlock lid.

3. Remove fish and broccoli to plates and serve immediately.

Dairy-Free Creamed Crab

Although this recipe is insanely good by the spoonful on its own, use this to level-up some simple dishes. Serve this crab atop a cod fillet with some fresh asparagus or even next to a grilled steak for a little surf and turf.

- **Hands-On Time: 5 minutes**
- **Cook Time: 5 minutes**

Serves 4

¼ cup ghee
½ stalk celery, finely diced
¼ cup finely diced red onion
1 pound lump crabmeat
¼ cup chicken broth
¼ cup unsweetened almond milk
2 teaspoons cassava flour
½ teaspoon sea salt
½ teaspoon freshly ground black pepper

WHAT KIND OF CRAB SHOULD YOU CHOOSE?

Fresh, lump crabmeat is the best option for this recipe—but it can be pricey. Fortunately, there are many different varieties and sections of the crab that can be purchased at a lower price point. It is even sold in cans like the more familiar tuna. Although there is imitation krab available, draw the line at that. It is stringy and packed with starch and chemicals.

1 Press the Sauté button on the Instant Pot®. Add ghee and melt. Add celery and red onion; stir-fry 3–5 minutes until celery begins to soften.

2 Stir crabmeat and broth into pot. Lock lid. Press the Steam button and adjust time to 0 minutes. When timer beeps, quick-release pressure until float valve drops and then unlock lid.

3 Carefully stir in milk, flour, salt, and pepper. Transfer to a serving bowl. Let set 5–10 minutes until thickened. Serve warm.

Citrus-Steamed Littleneck Clams

The citrus of the lemon and the richness of the chardonnay play so nicely against the brininess of the littleneck clams. This dish is a light and ideal lunch for a beautiful summer day. And, the good news is, you'll have chardonnay leftover from the recipe to enjoy a crisp glass of wine with your meal.

- **Hands-On Time: 5 minutes**
- **Cook Time: 8 minutes**

Serves 4

1 tablespoon avocado oil
2 shallots, diced
1 clove garlic, quartered
½ cup chardonnay
2 medium lemons
½ cup water
2 pounds fresh clams, rinsed
    and purged
½ cup chopped fresh Italian
    flat-leaf parsley

HOW DO YOU PURGE CLAMS?
To purge your clams of any residual sand, soak your clams in water with 1–2 tablespoons of cornmeal for 20 minutes. Scrub, rinse, and drain until there is no more sand.

1 Press the Sauté button on the Instant Pot®. Heat oil. Add shallots and sauté 3–5 minutes until translucent. Add garlic and cook 1 minute.

2 Add wine, juice of 1 lemon, and water to pot. Insert clams. Lock lid. Press the Manual or Pressure Cook button and adjust time to 2 minutes. When timer beeps, quick-release pressure until float valve drops and then unlock lid.

3 Transfer clams to four serving bowls and top with a generous scoop of cooking liquid and parsley. Serve a quarter of lemon with each bowl. Discard any clams that do not open.

Salmon Croquettes

Traditionally, croquettes are a fried delicacy, as the word *croquette* comes from the French word *croquer*, which literally means "to crunch" or "to be crunchy." However, in this recipe, you'll get all the flavors without the unhealthy cooking style. Serve as is, on a salad, or make a drizzle of Horseradish-Lemon Aioli.

- **Hands-On Time: 10 minutes**
- **Cook Time: 10 minutes**

Yields 16 croquettes

1 (14.75-ounce) can salmon

1 large egg

2 teaspoons prepared horseradish

1 tablespoon chopped dill

¼ cup almond meal

2 tablespoons finely diced celery

1 teaspoon sea salt

¼ teaspoon freshly ground black pepper

2 tablespoons avocado oil, divided

½ cup water

HOW TO MAKE HORSERADISH-LEMON AIOLI

Whip this up in a pinch to elevate your salmon croquettes. Whisk together ¼ cup mayonnaise, 2 teaspoons horseradish, 1 teaspoon lemon zest, a squeeze lemon juice, and a pinch or two of salt.

1. In a medium bowl, combine salmon, egg, horseradish, dill, almond meal, celery, salt, and pepper. Form into 16 oval-shaped croquettes (similar to the shape of a tater tot). Set aside.

2. Press the Sauté button on the Instant Pot® and heat 1 tablespoon oil. Place 8 croquettes around the edges of the pot. Sear all sides of the croquettes for a total of about 4 minutes. Remove the first batch and set aside. Add remaining oil and croquettes and sear 4 minutes. Remove croquettes.

3. Add water to the Instant Pot® and insert steamer basket. Place croquettes evenly on steamer basket. Lock lid. Press the Manual or Pressure Cook button and adjust time to 2 minutes. When timer beeps, quick-release pressure until float valve drops and then unlock lid.

4. Transfer croquettes and sauce to bowls and serve warm with sauce.

Greek Sea Bass

The flavors of the Mediterranean are spotlighted in this simple yet elegant dish. The richness of the olive oil, the freshness of the basil and tomatoes, and the brininess of the Kalamata olives all come together to dress up these already buttery pieces of sea bass.

- **Hands-On Time: 5 minutes**
- **Cook Time: 3 minutes**

Serves 2

2 (5-ounce) sea bass fillets

2 teaspoons olive oil, divided

1½ teaspoons sea salt, divided

10 pitted Kalamata olives, halved and divided

10 grape tomatoes, halved and divided

3 tablespoons chopped fresh basil leaves, divided

1 Place each fish fillet on a separate 10" × 10" square of aluminum foil. Drizzle each with 1 teaspoon olive oil. Sprinkle each with ½ teaspoon salt. Scatter olives and tomatoes evenly over each fillet. Top each with 1 tablespoon basil. Fold up the sides of each foil piece and crimp at the top to create foil packets.

2 Place both foil packets in the Instant Pot®. Lock lid. Press the Manual or Pressure Cook button and adjust time to 3 minutes. When timer beeps, quick-release pressure until float valve drops and then unlock lid.

3 Remove foil packets and transfer fish and toppings to two plates. Garnish each plate with equal amounts of remaining 1 tablespoon basil and ½ teaspoon salt.

Herbed Cod with Yellow Squash

The flavorful herb sauce is a fresh, creamy topping for the firm and flaky cod. The squash is a savory companion filled with vitamins A and C, potassium, and fiber. The steam in the Instant Pot® keeps this a moist and quick dish to make in a snap.

- **Hands-On Time: 10 minutes**
- **Cook Time: 3 minutes**

Serves 2

Herb Sauce
¼ cup mayonnaise
½ teaspoon fresh lemon juice
¼ teaspoon lemon zest
2 teaspoons Italian seasoning
1 small shallot, peeled and minced
Pinch sea salt
¼ teaspoon freshly ground black pepper

Cod and Squash
2 (6-ounce) cod fillets
½ teaspoon sea salt
1 cup water
1 large yellow squash, sliced into ¼" circles

1 In a small bowl, combine mayonnaise, lemon juice, lemon zest, Italian seasoning, shallot, salt, and pepper. Refrigerate covered until ready to use.

2 Season cod with salt.

3 Add water to the Instant Pot® and insert steamer basket. Place squash evenly on basket. Set cod atop squash. Lock lid. Press the Manual or Pressure Cook button and adjust time to 3 minutes. When timer beeps, let pressure release naturally for 2 minutes. Quick-release any remaining pressure until float valve drops and then unlock lid.

4 Transfer fish and squash to plates. Place a spoonful of the herb sauce on each cod fillet. Serve warm.

Mahi-Mahi with a Lemon-Caper Butter Sauce

Mahi-mahi is a firm fish that works well as a vessel for whatever flavors you cook it with. It is mild in taste and doesn't have that "fishy" flavor that you get when you use tuna or salmon.

- **Hands-On Time: 5 minutes**
- **Cook Time: 4 minutes**

Serves 2

2 (6-ounce, 1"-thick) mahi-mahi fillets

2 tablespoons fresh lemon juice

2 tablespoons capers

1 teaspoon sea salt

1 teaspoon lemon zest

2 tablespoons ghee

1 tablespoon chopped fresh Italian flat-leaf parsley

1 Place a piece of foil on the Instant Pot®'s steamer basket. Set both fillets on the foil. Create a "boat" with the foil by bringing up the edges. Pour lemon juice on fish, add capers, and season with salt and zest. Add a tablespoon of ghee on top of each fillet.

2 Insert steamer basket with fish into the Instant Pot®. Lock lid. Press the Manual or Pressure Cook button and adjust time to 4 minutes. Quick-release pressure until float valve drops and then unlock lid.

3 Transfer fish to two plates. Garnish each with ½ tablespoon chopped parsley and serve warm.

Steamed Snow Crab Legs

These crab legs are great served with melted ghee and plenty of lemon wedges. The wedges are not only great squeezed over the freshly cracked crab meat, but they act as a great hand cleaner and odor remover once you are done with this very interactive meal.

- **Hands-On Time: 5 minutes**
- **Cook Time: 3 minutes**

Serves 2

1 cup water

4 cloves garlic, quartered

1 tablespoon Old Bay Seasoning

1 bay leaf

2 pounds snow crab legs

1 Add water, garlic, Old Bay Seasoning, and bay leaf to the Instant Pot® and stir to combine.

2 Insert trivet in pot and add crab legs. Lock lid. Press the Steam button and adjust time to 3 minutes. When timer beeps, quick-release pressure until float valve drops and then unlock lid.

3 Transfer crab legs to a serving platter. Serve warm.

Simply Steamed Lobster Tails

There is no need to dress this up. Lobster tails and some melted ghee is simply divine together. Full of essential vitamins, lobster is a great source of protein and is low in calories and saturated fat.

- **Hands-On Time: 2 minutes**
- **Cook Time: 4 minutes**

Serves 4

1 cup water
4 small lobster tails
¼ cup ghee, melted

1 Add water to the Instant Pot® and insert steamer basket. Add lobster tails. Lock lid. Press the Steam button and adjust time to 4 minutes. When timer beeps, quick-release pressure until float valve drops and then unlock lid.

2 Remove lobster tails from pot and remove meat from shells. Serve with melted ghee.

MAKING BROTH WITH THE LOBSTER TAIL SHELLS

Don't just discard those empty lobster tail shells. Place the shells in the Instant Pot® with 4 cups water, 1 diced yellow onion, 1 peeled and diced carrot, and 1 diced stalk celery. Press the Manual or Pressure Cook button and adjust time to 30 minutes. When timer beeps, let pressure release naturally until float valve drops and then unlock lid. Use a slotted spoon to remove and discard the solids from the broth. Strain the remaining liquid through a fine-mesh sieve or cheesecloth. Refrigerate broth up to 4 days or freeze up to 6 months.

Quick Crawfish Boil

Fresh corn is not strictly a "no" paleo item. However, if you don't allow this in your diet, just skip it, as the recipe will still stand up without it.

- **Hands-On Time: 5 minutes**
- **Cook Time: 5 minutes**

Serves 4

1 large sweet onion, peeled, halved, and sliced in half-moons

2 ears corn, husked and halved

12-ounces precooked andouille sausage, cut into 1" pieces

2 pounds crawfish

2 tablespoons Old Bay Seasoning

1 (12-ounce) gluten-free beer

½ cup water

1. Layer onions evenly in the bottom of the Instant Pot®. Add corn and sausage in even layers. Add the crawfish and sprinkle with Old Bay Seasoning. Pour in beer and water. Lock lid. Press the Manual button and adjust time to 5 minutes. When timer beeps, quick-release pressure until float valve drops and then unlock lid.

2. Use a slotted spoon to transfer ingredients to a serving platter. Serve warm.

PACK A PICNIC

This Crawfish Boil is a great summer food. Line a picnic table with newspapers and pour all the ingredients onto the paper in the middle of the table. Guests can enjoy this family-style with no real etiquette to the meal other than to have fun. Oh, and don't forget a roll or two of paper towels. This can get messy.

10

Sweet Treats and Drinks

Paleo folks are often criticized if they even think about putting any sugar in their mouths. Never mind that white refined stuff. How dare you indulge in raw honey, pure maple syrup, coconut sugar crystals, or molasses? Is sugar-shaming a thing? Sometimes it feels like it is in the paleo community. So, how about this: if you are 100 percent paleo, we are in awe of you. If you are in the 75 percent zone and indulge on occasion, then this is the chapter for you. You will find some cheat meals without all the guilt.

If you're like most people, you probably have a sweet tooth that pulls at your stomach from time to time. The great thing about the Instant Pot® is that it creates desserts that are just the right size to make your sweet tooth *and* your scale happy. Most of these desserts provide only 4–6 servings, so you won't be tempted to overeat and you won't have desserts hanging around your kitchen for days on end. There are also some drinks that are treats for you and your friends. And with recipes ranging from Upside-Down Peach Cobbler and Café Mocha Muffins to Homemade Chai Tea Latte and Gluhwein, these perfect sweet delights are guaranteed to hit the spot...no matter what you find yourself craving.

Spiced Applesauce

After a day of apple picking, applesauce is a perfect solution for your haul. Pick a variety for a balanced flavor...also, keep those apple skins on during cooking as they lend a beautiful hue to the finished product!

- **Hands-On Time: 20 minutes**
- **Cook Time: 8 minutes**

Yields 10 cups

4 pounds variety of apples, cored and chopped

1 cinnamon stick

2 whole star anise

6 whole allspice

½ cup freshly squeezed orange juice

⅓ cup honey

½ teaspoon sea salt

⅓ cup water

1 Add the apples, cinnamon stick, star anise, whole allspice, orange juice, honey, salt, and water to the Instant Pot®. (Alternatively, add the cinnamon stick, star anise, and whole allspice to a spice bag for easy retrieval after cooking.)

2 Press the Manual or Pressure Cook button and adjust time to 8 minutes. When timer beeps, quick-release pressure until float valve drops and then unlock lid.

3 Remove cinnamon stick, star anise, and whole allspice.

4 Use an immersion blender to blend the ingredients in the pot until desired consistency is reached.

Café Mocha Muffins

Either for desserts, breakfast-on-the-go, or just a snack, these Café Mocha Muffins are the perfect bite for any coffee and chocolate lover!

- **Hands-On Time: 10 minutes**
- **Cook Time: 9 minutes**

Serves 6

⅔ cup cassava flour

¼ cup unsweetened cocoa powder

2 teaspoons instant espresso powder

2 teaspoons baking powder

½ teaspoon baking soda

Pinch sea salt

½ teaspoon vanilla extract

3 tablespoons ghee, melted

2 large eggs

2 tablespoons unsweetened almond milk

⅓ cup pure maple syrup

1 cup water

1   In a large bowl, combine flour, cocoa, espresso powder, baking powder, baking soda, and sea salt.

2   In a medium bowl, combine vanilla, ghee, eggs, almond milk, and syrup.

3   Pour wet ingredients from the medium bowl into the large bowl with dry ingredients. Gently combine ingredients. Do not overmix. Spoon mixture into 6 lightly greased silicone cupcake liners.

4   Pour water into the Instant Pot® and insert trivet or steamer basket. Place cupcake liners on top. Lock lid. Press the Manual or Pressure Cook button and adjust time to 9 minutes. When timer beeps, quick-release pressure until float valve drops and then unlock lid.

5   Remove muffins from pot and set aside to cool 5 minutes.

Strawberry Cupcakes with Chocolate Ganache

Everyone loves the combination of strawberries and chocolate and this perfect combo is neatly put together and delivered to you in a scrumptious little cupcake. Gluten? Who needs that! You won't even miss the stuff with each heavenly bite!

- **Hands-On Time: 10 minutes**
- **Cook Time: 10 minutes**

Serves 6

Strawberry Cupcakes
1¼ cups cassava flour
2 teaspoons baking powder
½ teaspoon baking soda
Pinch sea salt
½ teaspoon vanilla extract
1 teaspoon lime zest
3 tablespoons ghee, melted
2 large eggs
⅓ cup pure maple syrup
⅓ cup finely diced
   strawberries
1 cup water

Chocolate Ganache
3½-ounce dark chocolate bar
1 teaspoon pure maple syrup
Pinch sea salt
½ cup unsweetened almond
   milk
2 teaspoons coconut palm
   shortening

1. In a large bowl, combine flour, baking powder, baking soda, and sea salt.

2. In a medium bowl, combine vanilla, lime zest, ghee, eggs, and syrup.

3. Pour wet ingredients from the medium bowl into the large bowl with dry ingredients. Gently combine ingredients. Do not overmix. Fold in strawberries. Spoon mixture into 6 lightly greased silicone cupcake liners.

4. Pour water into the Instant Pot® and insert trivet or steamer basket. Place cupcake liners on top. Lock lid. Press the Manual or Pressure Cook button and adjust time to 9 minutes. When timer beeps, quick-release pressure until float valve drops and then unlock lid.

5. Remove cupcakes from pot and set aside to cool 5 minutes.

6. Once cupcakes have cooled, prepare ganache. In a small bowl, break up the chocolate bar into pieces. Add syrup and salt. Set aside. Add milk and shortening to a small saucepan and heat over medium. Bring to a rolling boil. Pour milk mixture over chocolate and whisk until smooth.

7. Dip tops of cupcakes in ganache and place on a cooling rack. Serve.

Apple Brown Betty

The Brown Betty goes back to the mid-1800s in America and was traditionally made with bread slices or cracker crumbs. *King of the Hill* fans know that Peggy is very proud of her Apple Brown Betty and loves to share. This Instant Pot® version takes out the grains but doesn't skimp on taste. Share this with your family. Share this with your neighbors!

- **Hands-On Time: 15 minutes**
- **Cook Time: 18 minutes**

Serves 6

Crust
1 cup cassava flour
2 teaspoons baking powder
½ teaspoon baking soda
¼ teaspoon ground
    cinnamon
Pinch sea salt
½ teaspoon vanilla extract
2 tablespoons ghee, melted
2 large eggs
2 tablespoons honey

Apple Betty
2 tablespoons ghee
3 medium apples, cored,
    peeled, and thinly sliced
2 tablespoons molasses
1 teaspoon orange zest
½ teaspoon ground cinnamon
¼ cup chopped walnuts
2 cups water

1 Lightly grease a 7-inch springform pan. Set aside.

2 In a large bowl, combine flour, baking powder, baking soda, cinnamon, and salt.

3 In a medium bowl, combine vanilla, melted ghee, eggs, and honey.

4 Pour wet ingredients from the medium bowl into the large bowl with dry ingredients. Gently combine ingredients. Do not overmix. Set aside.

5 Press the Sauté button on the Instant Pot® and heat ghee. Add apples and toss. Cook about 3 minutes to remove some water from the apples. Use a slotted spoon to transfer the apples to a medium bowl. Toss in molasses, orange zest, and cinnamon. Evenly transfer to greased springform pan. Sprinkle chopped walnuts over apple mixture.

6 Spoon in crust mixture and spread evenly to edges of pan.

7 Pour water into the Instant Pot® and insert trivet or steamer basket. Place springform pan on top. Lock lid. Press the Manual or Pressure Cook button and adjust time to 15 minutes. When timer beeps, quick-release pressure until float valve drops and then unlock lid.

8 Remove pan from pot and refrigerate at least 30 minutes to allow the dessert to set. Unlock springform pan. Flip onto a serving plate and remove springform plate. Serve.

Upside-Down Peach Cobbler

This Peach Cobbler could show up to any Georgia dinner party and fit right in (other than the fact that it only serves four!). The Instant Pot® version of Peach Cobbler requires frozen peaches, so you can enjoy this dessert any time of the year. Also, you can make this at the last minute without worrying about cutting peaches or defrosting freezer items.

- **Hands-On Time: 10 minutes**
- **Cook Time: 15 minutes**

Serves 4

1 pound bag frozen sliced peaches
1 tablespoon honey
2 tablespoons ghee, softened
½ teaspoon ground cinnamon
1 cup cassava flour
2 teaspoons baking powder
½ teaspoon baking soda
Pinch sea salt
½ teaspoon vanilla extract
2 tablespoons ghee, melted
2 large eggs
¼ cup pure maple syrup
2 cups water

1   Lightly grease a 7-inch springform pan. Scatter frozen sliced peaches in an even layer. Drizzle with honey. Place pats of softened ghee over peaches. Sprinkle evenly with cinnamon.

2   In a large bowl, combine flour, baking powder, baking soda, and salt.

3   In a medium bowl, combine vanilla, melted ghee, eggs, and syrup.

4   Pour wet ingredients from the medium bowl into the large bowl with dry ingredients. Gently combine ingredients. Do not overmix. Carefully and evenly smooth sticky batter over peaches.

5   Pour water into the Instant Pot® and insert trivet or steamer basket. Place springform pan on top. Lock lid. Press the Manual or Pressure Cook button and adjust time to 15 minutes. When timer beeps, quick-release pressure until float valve drops and then unlock lid.

6   Remove pan from pot and refrigerate at least 30 minutes to allow the cake to set. Unlock springform pan. Flip onto a serving plate and remove springform plate. Serve.

Banana Pudding Cake

Banana pudding is a Southern tradition, but sometimes you just need a quick version so that you have extra time to gossip with your friends.

- **Hands-On Time: 15 minutes**
- **Cook Time: 15 minutes**

Serves 4

Vanilla Cake
1 cup cassava flour
2 teaspoons baking powder
½ teaspoon baking soda
Pinch sea salt
1 teaspoon vanilla extract
2 tablespoons ghee, melted
2 large eggs
2 tablespoons honey

Banana Pudding
2 medium ripe bananas, sliced
2 large egg yolks
1 tablespoon pure maple syrup
¼ teaspoon vanilla extract
Pinch sea salt
¾ cup unsweetened almond milk
2 cups water

1 Lightly grease a 7-inch springform pan. Set aside.

2 In a large bowl, combine flour, baking powder, baking soda, and salt.

3 In a medium bowl, combine vanilla, ghee, eggs, and honey.

4 Pour wet ingredients from the medium bowl into the large bowl with dry ingredients. Gently mix to combine ingredients. Do not overmix. Set cake mixture aside.

5 Evenly distribute bananas on the bottom of the prepared springform pan.

6 In a small bowl, whisk together egg yolks, maple syrup, vanilla, and salt. Set aside. In saucepan over medium-low heat, heat almond milk to a low simmer. Whisk a spoonful of the milk into the egg mixture to temper the eggs, and then slowly whisk that egg mixture into the saucepan with remaining almond milk. Pour this pudding layer evenly over bananas. Refrigerate 10 minutes.

7 Carefully spoon cake mixture over pudding layer and spread evenly to edges of pan.

8 Pour water into the Instant Pot® and insert trivet or steamer basket. Place springform pan on top. Lock lid. Press the Manual or Pressure Cook button and adjust time to 15 minutes. When timer beeps, quick-release pressure until float valve drops and then unlock lid.

9 Remove pan from pot and refrigerate at least 30 minutes to allow the dessert to set. Unlock springform pan. Flip onto a serving plate and remove springform plate. Serve.

Chocolate Chip Zucchini Bread

Loaded with nutritional zucchini and sweetened with a little honey and dates, this is the perfect bread for a sweet tooth. Enjoy with a warm cup of coffee or tea for a quiet morning curled up with a great book.

- **Hands-On Time: 15 minutes**
- **Cook Time: 15 minutes**

Serves 6

1½ cups cassava flour
1 teaspoon ground cinnamon
⅛ teaspoon ground nutmeg
2 teaspoons baking powder
½ teaspoon baking soda
Pinch sea salt
⅓ cup finely diced pitted dates
3 large eggs
2 cups grated zucchini (about 2 small zucchini)
1 teaspoon vanilla extract
¼ cup ghee, melted
⅓ cup honey
½ cup chopped pecans
¼ cup dark chocolate chips
2 cups water

1. Lightly grease a 7-inch springform pan. Set aside.

2. In a large bowl, combine flour, cinnamon, nutmeg, baking powder, baking soda, salt, and dates.

3. In a medium bowl, combine eggs, zucchini, vanilla, ghee, and honey.

4. Pour wet ingredients from the medium bowl into the large bowl with dry ingredients. Gently combine ingredients. Fold in pecans and chocolate chips. Do not overmix. Spoon mixture into springform pan.

5. Pour water into the Instant Pot® and insert trivet. Place springform pan on top. Lock lid. Press the Manual or Pressure Cook button and adjust time to 15 minutes. When timer beeps, quick-release pressure until float valve drops and then unlock lid.

6. Remove pan from the Instant Pot®. Let rest 15 minutes. Use a paper towel to dab off any excess moisture. Open pan and cut and serve.

Double Chocolate Custard

What is better than chocolate? Double chocolate! Egg yolks are not only nature's sauce once poached, but they add such a richness to custards and ice creams. The chocolate enhances this richness. You won't believe that this is paleo and dairy-free. Oh, but it is. So simple. So luxurious.

- **Hands-On Time: 10 minutes**
- **Cook Time: 15 minutes**

Serves 4

4 large egg yolks
¼ cup honey
Pinch sea salt
¼ teaspoon vanilla extract
2 tablespoons unsweetened cocoa powder
1½ cups unsweetened almond milk
¼ cup dark chocolate chips
2 cups water

1 In a small bowl, whisk together egg yolks, honey, salt, vanilla, and cocoa. Set aside.

2 In saucepan over medium-low heat, heat almond milk to a low simmer. Whisk a spoonful of the milk into the egg mixture to temper the eggs, and then slowly whisk that egg mixture into the saucepan with remaining almond milk. Add chocolate chips and continually stir on simmer until chocolate is melted, about 10 minutes. Remove from heat and evenly distribute chocolate mixture among four custard ramekins.

3 Pour water into the Instant Pot® and insert trivet. Place ramekins onto trivet. Lock lid. Press the Manual or Pressure Cook button and adjust time to 5 minutes. When timer beeps, let pressure release naturally for 15 minutes. Quick-release any remaining pressure until float valve drops and then unlock lid.

4 Transfer custards to a plate and refrigerate covered overnight to allow the custard to set. Serve.

Coconut Key Lime Custard

Hello Key West! Although the little flavorful key limes are preferred in this recipe, if it isn't the season, feel free to use standard limes. Either way, close your eyes and you'll be transported to Alabama Jack's while wearing your flip-flops and tank top. Don't forget to go enjoy that glorious sunset over the ocean...at least in your dreams.

- **Hands-On Time: 10 minutes**
- **Cook Time: 15 minutes**

Serves 4

4 large egg yolks
¼ cup honey
Pinch sea salt
¼ teaspoon vanilla extract
⅓ cup fresh key lime juice
1 teaspoon key lime zest
1½ cups canned coconut milk
2 cups water

1 In a small bowl, whisk together egg yolks, honey, salt, vanilla, lime juice, and lime zest. Set aside.

2 In saucepan over medium-low heat, heat coconut milk to a low simmer. Whisk a spoonful of the milk into the egg mixture to temper the eggs, and then slowly whisk that egg mixture into the saucepan with remaining coconut milk. Continually stir on simmer about 10 minutes. Remove from heat and evenly distribute custard mixture among four ramekins.

3 Pour water into the Instant Pot® and insert trivet. Place ramekins onto trivet. Lock lid. Press the Manual or Pressure Cook button and adjust time to 5 minutes. When timer beeps, let pressure release naturally for 15 minutes. Quick-release any remaining pressure until float valve drops and then unlock lid.

4 Transfer custards to a plate and refrigerate covered overnight to allow the custard to fully set. Serve.

Grain-Free Stuffed Apples

You can have your apples and stuff them too! After a day of apple picking with the family, this glorious traditional recipe can be cooked and on your plates within 15 minutes. Serve with a scoop of vanilla or cinnamon ice cream to take it over the top!

- **Hands-On Time: 10 minutes**
- **Cook Time: 5 minutes**

Serves 4

3 tablespoons ghee, softened

2 tablespoons pumpkin purée

1 teaspoon ground cinnamon

¼ cup chopped pecans

2 tablespoons unsweetened coconut flakes

2 teaspoons pure maple syrup

Pinch sea salt

4 medium cooking apples

1 cup water

1 In a small bowl, mix together ghee, pumpkin purée, cinnamon, pecans, coconut flakes, syrup, and salt. Set aside.

2 Rinse and dry the apples. Cut the tops off the apples. Hollow out and core the apples by cutting to, but not through, the apple bottoms.

3 Place each apple on a piece of aluminum foil that is large enough to wrap the apple completely. Fill the apple centers with prepared mixture. Wrap the foil around each apple, folding the foil over at the top and then pinching it firmly together.

4 Pour water into the Instant Pot® and insert trivet. Place the wrapped apples on the rack. Lock lid. Press the Manual or Pressure Cook button and adjust time to 5 minutes. When timer beeps, let pressure release naturally for 10 minutes. Quick-release any remaining pressure until float valve drops and then unlock lid.

5 Carefully unwrap apples and transfer to serving plates.

Hummingbird Cake

Hummingbird Cake is a Southern spice cake filled with banana, pineapple, and nuts. Traditionally, there is a rich white frosting with coconut flakes...it really is what dreams are made of. This recipe cuts out that thick frosting but doesn't skimp on any of the flavor. It makes for a great after-dinner dessert enjoyed with a cup of coffee.

- **Hands-On Time: 15 minutes**
- **Cook Time: 15 minutes**

Serves 4

¾ cup cassava flour
2 teaspoons baking powder
½ teaspoon baking soda
½ teaspoon ground cinnamon
Pinch sea salt
¼ teaspoon vanilla extract
2 tablespoons ghee, melted
2 large eggs
¼ cup undrained crushed pineapple
¼ cup mashed banana (about 1 small banana)
2 tablespoons pure maple syrup
¼ cup chopped pecans
2 cups water

Topping

1 tablespoon pure maple syrup
3 tablespoons unsweetened coconut flakes, divided

1 Lightly grease a 6-inch cake pan. Set aside.

2 In a large bowl, combine flour, baking powder, baking soda, cinnamon, and sea salt.

3 In a medium bowl, combine vanilla, ghee, eggs, pineapple, banana, and syrup.

4 Pour wet ingredients from the medium bowl into the large bowl with dry ingredients. Gently combine ingredients. Do not overmix. Fold in pecans. Spoon mixture into greased cake pan.

5 Pour water into the Instant Pot® and insert trivet or steamer basket. Place cake pan on top. Lock lid. Press the Manual or Pressure Cook button and adjust time to 15 minutes. When timer beeps, quick-release pressure until float valve drops and then unlock lid.

6 Remove pan from pot and set aside to cool 5 minutes. Flip cake onto a serving plate.

7 In a small bowl, combine syrup with 2 tablespoons coconut flakes. Spread on the top of the cake. Garnish with the remaining 1 tablespoon coconut flakes.

Poached Cherries

If you are overrun with cherries, poach them! They are a nice light dessert to quench that sweet tooth. Or serve them over some dairy-free ice cream or grain-free cake. And if you enjoy cherries, invest in a pitter. It will be one of the few gadgets that get some use, unlike the others in the graveyard of never-used kitchen tools.

- **Hands-On Time: 10 minutes**
- **Cook Time: 15 minutes**

Serves 4

2 cups water

½ cup pure maple syrup

Zest and juice from 1 medium orange

2 teaspoons vanilla extract

1 pound sweet cherries, pitted

1 cinnamon stick

1   Add all ingredients to the Instant Pot®. Press the Manual or Pressure Cook button and adjust time to 5 minutes. When timer beeps, let pressure release naturally for 15 minutes. Quick-release any remaining pressure until float valve drops and then unlock lid. Discard cinnamon stick.

2   Transfer cherries to an airtight container and refrigerate until ready to eat, warm or cold.

Upside-Down Chocolate Cherry Cake

Chocolate covered cherries are a no-brainer combination, so this cake just makes sense. A seasonal treat, pick up one of those fresh sweet cherry bags that you see in the grocery store once a year and this is your dessert. Rich, brownie-like chocolate cake and naturally sweet pitted cherries, this should satisfy any sweet tooth without breaking the calorie bank.

- **Hands-On Time: 15 minutes**
- **Cook Time: 15 minutes**

Serves 4

16 fresh sweet cherries, halved and pitted
⅔ cup cassava flour
⅓ cup unsweetened cocoa powder
2 teaspoons baking powder
½ teaspoon baking soda
Pinch sea salt
½ teaspoon vanilla extract
3 tablespoons ghee, melted
2 large eggs
2 tablespoons unsweetened almond milk
⅓ cup pure maple syrup
2 cups water

1 Lightly grease a 6-inch cake pan. Place cherries, flat side down, into cake pan until the bottom of the pan is covered. Set aside.

2 In a large bowl, combine flour, cocoa, baking powder, baking soda, and sea salt.

3 In a medium bowl, combine vanilla, ghee, eggs, milk, and syrup.

4 Pour wet ingredients from the medium bowl into the large bowl with dry ingredients. Gently combine ingredients. Do not overmix. Spoon mixture into greased cake pan.

5 Pour water into the Instant Pot® and insert trivet or steamer basket. Place cake pan on top. Lock lid. Press the Manual or Pressure Cook button and adjust time to 15 minutes. When timer beeps, quick-release pressure until float valve drops and then unlock lid.

6 Remove pan from pot and set aside to cool for 5 minutes. Flip cake onto a serving plate.

Mixed Berry Quick Jam

If you go down the jam and jelly aisle and look at the ingredients' label, you will notice that the jars are filled with refined sugars and preservatives. Enjoy this jam with whatever berries you have on-hand after a day of berry picking with the family.

- **Hands-On Time: 5 minutes**
- **Cook Time: 1 minute**

Yields 3 cups

2 cups blueberries
2 cups sliced strawberries
1 cup freshly squeezed
    orange juice
2 teaspoons orange zest
½ cup honey
Pinch sea salt

1 Place all ingredients in the Instant Pot®. Lock lid. Press the Manual or Pressure Cook button and adjust time to 1 minute. When timer beeps, let pressure release naturally until float valve drops and then unlock lid.

2 Use an immersion blender to blend the ingredients in the pot until desired consistency is reached. Spoon into a lidded container and store in refrigerator. Use within 2 weeks.

Quick Lime Marmalade

For a sweet-bitter-tart treat, this quick marmalade is for you. It can be used on gluten-free scones and biscuits, frozen into ice cubes for amazing additions to your gin drinks, or throw in a small spoonful to your Thai coconut milk–based dishes.

- **Hands-On Time: 10 minutes**
- **Cook Time: 10 minutes**

Serves 10

6 medium limes
½ cup honey
Pinch sea salt
½ cup water

1 Prepare limes by scrubbing the outside and removing any possible shiny wax on the exterior. Thinly slice limes, the thinner the better. Discard seeds. Cut slices in half.

2 Place all ingredients in the Instant Pot®. Lock lid. Press the Manual or Pressure Cook button and adjust time to 10 minutes. When timer beeps, let pressure release naturally until float valve drops and then unlock lid. If mixture is too watery, let simmer unlidded until desired consistency.

3 Transfer mixture to a lidded jar and refrigerate. Use within 2 weeks or freeze into cubes for later use.

Fresh-Brewed Arnie Palmer

Named after the beloved American golfer, Arnold Palmer, this summertime drink combines simple brewed tea with fresh, sweet and tart lemonade. If you'd like to adult this drink up, add a shot of vodka or limoncello to the finished product...but then you call it a John Daly!

- **Hands-On Time: 5 minutes**
- **Cook Time: 15 minutes**

Serves 4

4 medium lemons, halved
5 tea bags
7 cups water
½ cup honey

1 Juice lemons. Discard seeds but keep the rinds.

2 Place lemon juice, lemon rinds, tea bags, and water in Instant Pot®. Lock lid. Press the Steam button and adjust time to 10 minutes. When timer beeps, quick-release pressure until float valve drops and then unlock lid.

3 Add honey and let steep an additional 5 minutes. Strain. Press any additional liquid and flavor out of the tea bags. Serve over ice.

Gluhwein

Gluhwein is a glorious warm spiced wine drink that you sip while walking around the Christmas Markets in Germany. It is cold, yet the warm Gluhwein and the beautiful woodcrafts pull a person into the holiday. Share this enchanting drink with your stateside friends to introduce them to the warmth.

- **Hands-On Time: 5 minutes**
- **Cook Time: 10 minutes**

Serves 6

1 (750-milliliter) bottle dry red wine
½ medium lemon, quartered
1 medium orange, quartered
½ cup honey
4 whole cloves
2 cardamom pods
1 cinnamon stick
1 whole star anise

1 Add all ingredients to the Instant Pot®. Lock lid. Press the Steam button and adjust time to 10 minutes. When timer beeps, quick-release pressure until float valve drops and then unlock lid.

2 Using a fine-mesh sieve or cheesecloth, strain out solids. Serve warm.

Homemade Chai Tea Latte

Your friends will think they just stopped by their local favorite teahouse when they taste the freshness and richness of this homemade chai. Sweetened with maple syrup instead of refined sugars and made creamy with unsweetened almond milk instead of heavy cream, this drink's facelift is one to be savored.

- **Hands-On Time: 5 minutes**
- **Cook Time: 15 minutes**

Serves 4

5 cups water
4 black tea bags
3 cardamom pods
4 whole cloves
1 cinnamon stick
4 whole allspice
¼ teaspoon ground nutmeg
1 cup unsweetened almond milk
¼ cup pure maple syrup

WHAT IS A SPICE BAG?

In the recipe, the solids are free-floating; however, to avoid straining the hot liquid at the end of the cooking process, simply bind the cardamom pods, whole cloves, cinnamon stick, and whole allspice in a cheesecloth tied with butcher twine. Premade spice bags are also sold in specialty stores or found easily online.

1 Place water, tea bags, cardamom, cloves, cinnamon stick, allspice, and nutmeg in Instant Pot®. Lock lid. Press the Steam button and adjust time to 10 minutes. When timer beeps, quick-release pressure until float valve drops and then unlock lid.

2 Add milk and syrup and let steep an additional 5 minutes. Strain. Press any additional liquid and flavor out of the tea bags. Serve warm, chilled, or on ice.

Spiced Mocha Latte

Why waste those dollars when you can whip up this concoction on your own with minimal effort? Pour the finished product in your to-go coffee mug and know that you have a cheaper and healthier product to wake you up and take you down the road without killing your wallet.

- **Hands-On Time: 5 minutes**
- **Cook Time: 15 minutes**

Serves 4

4 cups water

2 tablespoons instant espresso coffee powder

2 tablespoons unsweetened cocoa powder

Pinch sea salt

4 whole allspice

1 star anise

4 cardamom pods

1 cinnamon stick

2 cups unsweetened almond milk

½ cup pure maple syrup

1 Add water, espresso, cocoa, salt, allspice, star anise, cardamom, and cinnamon stick in the Instant Pot®. Lock lid. Press the Steam button and adjust time to 10 minutes. When timer beeps, quick-release pressure until float valve drops and then unlock lid.

2 Add milk and syrup and let steep an additional 5 minutes. Strain. Serve warm, chilled, or on ice.

Mexican Hot Cocoa

Rich, delicious, and warm, hot cocoa is what soothes the body after spending the morning shoveling snow out of the driveway with the family. Set this up in the Instant Pot® and it will be ready to be ladled into those mugs. Also, if you allow dairy in your life, whisk some organic cream with a little honey for a fluffy topping.

- **Hands-On Time: 5 minutes**
- **Cook Time: 8 minutes**

Serves 4

6 cups unsweetened almond milk
¼ cup unsweetened cocoa powder
1 (3½-ounce) dark chocolate bar, broken into pieces
¼ teaspoon chili powder
Pinch cayenne pepper
Pinch ground nutmeg
Pinch sea salt
1 cinnamon stick
2 teaspoons vanilla extract
¼ cup honey

1. Place all ingredients in the Instant Pot®. Lock lid. Press the Steam button and adjust time to 8 minutes. When timer beeps, quick-release pressure until float valve drops and then unlock lid.

2. Remove and discard cinnamon stick. Ladle cocoa into mugs and serve warm.

Appendix A
Paleo "Yes" and "No" Foods

In order to ensure your success on the Paleolithic diet, you need to stock your pantry with fresh, organic produce and grass-fed and barn-roaming meats. Feel free to experiment with items you would not normally choose. That will spice things up and keep you interested in the diet. Also listed here are the foods you should avoid, including processed grains, potatoes, legumes, and dairy.

PALEO "YES" FOODS

Protein
Alligator
Bass
Bear
Beef, lean and trimmed
Bison
Bluefish
Caribou
Chicken breast
Chuck steak
Clams
Cod
Crab
Crayfish
Egg whites
Eggs
Flank steak
Game hen breasts
Goat
Grouper
Haddock
Halibut
Hamburger, extra lean
Herring

Liver (beef, lamb, goat, or chicken)
Lobster
London broil
Mackerel
Marrow (beef, lamb, or goat)
Mussels
Orange roughy
Ostrich
Oysters
Pheasant
Pork chops
Pork loin
Pork, lean
Quail
Rabbit
Rattlesnake
Red snapper
Salmon, wild-caught
Scallops
Scrod
Shrimp
Tilapia

Tongue (beef, lamb, or goat)
Trout
Tuna, canned, unsalted
Tuna, fresh
Turkey breast
Veal, lean
Venison

Leafy Vegetables
Arugula
Beet greens
Bitterleaf
Bok choy
Broccoli rabe
Brussels sprouts
Cabbage
Celery
Chard
Chicory
Chinese cabbage
Collard greens
Dandelion
Endive

Fiddlehead

Kale

Lettuce

Radicchio

Spinach

Swiss chard

Turnip

Watercress

Yarrow

Fruiting Vegetables

Avocado

Bell pepper

Cucumber

Eggplant

Squash

Sweet pepper

Tomatillo

Tomato

Zucchini

Flowers and Flower Buds

Artichoke

Broccoli

Cauliflower

Bulb and Stem Vegetables

Asparagus

Celery

Florence fennel

Garlic

Kohlrabi

Leek

Onion

Sea Vegetables and Herbs of All Types

Fruits

Apple

Apricot

Banana

Blackberries

Blueberries

Cantaloupe

Cherries

Coconut

Cranberries (not dried)

Figs

Grapefruit

Grapes

Guava

Honeydew melon

Kiwi

Lemon

Lime

Mandarin orange

Mango

Nectarine

Orange

Papaya

Passion fruit

Peaches

Pears

Persimmon

Pineapple

Plums

Pomegranate

Raspberries

Rhubarb

Star fruit

Strawberries

Tangerine

Watermelon

All other fruits are acceptable

Fats, Nuts, Seeds, Oils, and Fatty Proteins

Almond butter

Almonds

Avocado

Brazil nuts

Canola oil

Cashew

Cashew butter

Chestnuts

Coconut oil

Flaxseed oil

Hazelnuts/filberts

Macadamia butter

Macadamia nuts

Olive oil

Pecans

Pine nuts

Pistachios

Pumpkin seeds

Safflower oil

Sesame seeds

Sunflower butter, unsweetened

Sunflower seeds

Udo's oil

Walnut oil

Walnuts

PALEO "NO" FOODS

Legume Vegetables

American groundnut

Azuki beans

Black-eyed peas

Chickpeas (garbanzo bean)

Common beans

Fava beans

Green beans

Guar

Indian peas

Kidney beans

Lentils

Lima beans

Mung beans

Navy beans

Okra

Peanut

Peanut butter

Peas

Pigeon peas

Pinto beans

Red beans

Rice beans

Snow peas

Soybean and soy products

String beans

Sugar snap peas

White beans

Dairy Foods

All processed foods made
with any dairy products

Butter

Cheese

Cream

Dairy spreads

Frozen yogurt

Ice cream

Ice milk

Low-fat milk

Nonfat dairy creamer

Powdered milk

Skim milk

Whole milk

Yogurt

Cereal Grains

Barley

Corn

Millet

Oats

Rice

Rye

Sorghum

Wheat

Wild rice

Cereal Grain-Like Seeds

Amaranth

Buckwheat

Quinoa

Starchy Vegetables

Starchy tubers (in large
quantities)

Manioc

Potatoes and all potato
products

Sweet potatoes or yams
(unless after workout to
replenish gylcogen)

Tapioca pudding

Salt-Containing Foods, Fatty Meats, and Sugar

Almost all commercial salad
dressings and condiments

Candy

Frankfurters

Processed meats

Salami

Salt

Salted nuts

Smoked, dried, and salted
fish and meat

Soft drinks and fruit juice

Sugar

Appendix B
US/Metric Conversion Chart

VOLUME CONVERSIONS

US Volume Measure	Metric Equivalent
⅛ teaspoon	0.5 milliliter
¼ teaspoon	1 milliliter
½ teaspoon	2 milliliters
1 teaspoon	5 milliliters
½ tablespoon	7 milliliters
1 tablespoon (3 teaspoons)	15 milliliters
2 tablespoons (1 fluid ounce)	30 milliliters
¼ cup (4 tablespoons)	60 milliliters
⅓ cup	90 milliliters
½ cup (4 fluid ounces)	125 milliliters
⅔ cup	160 milliliters
¾ cup (6 fluid ounces)	180 milliliters
1 cup (16 tablespoons)	250 milliliters
1 pint (2 cups)	500 milliliters
1 quart (4 cups)	1 liter (about)

WEIGHT CONVERSIONS

US Weight Measure	Metric Equivalent
½ ounce	15 grams
1 ounce	30 grams
2 ounces	60 grams
3 ounces	85 grams
¼ pound (4 ounces)	115 grams
½ pound (8 ounces)	225 grams
¾ pound (12 ounces)	340 grams
1 pound (16 ounces)	454 grams

OVEN TEMPERATURE CONVERSIONS

Degrees Fahrenheit	Degrees Celsius
200 degrees F	95 degrees C
250 degrees F	120 degrees C
275 degrees F	135 degrees C
300 degrees F	150 degrees C
325 degrees F	160 degrees C
350 degrees F	180 degrees C
375 degrees F	190 degrees C
400 degrees F	205 degrees C
425 degrees F	220 degrees C
450 degrees F	230 degrees C

BAKING PAN SIZES

American	Metric
8 x 1½ inch round baking pan	20 x 4 cm cake tin
9 x 1½ inch round baking pan	23 x 3.5 cm cake tin
11 x 7 x 1½ inch baking pan	28 x 18 x 4 cm baking tin
13 x 9 x 2 inch baking pan	30 x 20 x 5 cm baking tin
2 quart rectangular baking dish	30 x 20 x 3 cm baking tin
15 x 10 x 2 inch baking pan	30 x 25 x 2 cm baking tin (Swiss roll tin)
9 inch pie plate	22 x 4 or 23 x 4 cm pie plate
7 or 8 inch springform pan	18 or 20 cm springform or loose bottom cake tin
9 x 5 x 3 inch loaf pan	23 x 13 x 7 cm or 2 lb narrow loaf or pâté tin
1½ quart casserole	1.5 liter casserole
2 quart casserole	2 liter casserole

Index

Note: Page numbers in **bold** indicate recipe category lists.

About the Author

Michelle Fagone is a recipe developer, mother of two, and food blogger. On her site, CavegirlCuisine.com, Michelle shares recipes and knowledge about the health benefits of cooking with local, fresh, and unprocessed foods. Despite being a Southern gal at heart, her travel and food experiences as a Navy brat and current Army spouse have given her a unique appreciation for worldly flavors. While comfort is the basis for most of her recipes, you will often find a twist of exciting flavors and combinations that make her recipes not only appealing to a broad audience but uniquely delicious! CavegirlCuisine.com was named one of the Top 50 Paleo Blogs of 2012 by the Institute for the Psychology of Eating. Michelle lives in Louisville, Kentucky.